Why Workshop?

Why Workshop?

Changing Course
in 7–12 English

Edited by

Richard Bullock

Director of Writing Programs, Wright State University

 Stenhouse Publishers
York, Maine

Stenhouse Publishers, 431 York Street, York, Maine 03909
www.stenhouse.com

Library of Congress Cataloging-in-Publication Data

Why workshop? : changing course in 7–12 English / edited by Richard Bullock. p. cm. Includes bibliographical references (p.).
ISBN 1-57110-084-9 (alk. paper) 1. English language—Composition and exercises—Study and teaching (Secondary)—United States—Case studies. 2. Creative writing (Secondary education)—United States—Case studies. 3. Curriculum change—United States—Case studies. 4. Teachers' workshops—United States—Case studies. I. Bullock, Richard H.
LB1631.W384 1998 808'.042'0712—dc21 98-24010 CIP

Cover and interior design by Joyce C. Weston
Cover photograph by Jim Whitney
Typeset by Technologies 'N Typography

Manufactured in the United States of America on acid-free paper 03 02 01 00 99 98 9 8 7 6 5 4 3 2 1

Contents

Preface

Why Workshop? owes its existence to Change Course!, a summer program that brought twelve middle- and high-school English teachers to Wright State University's campus each July for five years. For a month, the teachers lived, ate, wrote, and studied together while participating in courses in writing, integrated language arts, and authentic assessment. By the end of the month they devised a plan for a course that, with their principal's blessing, they implemented the following school year. During that year they met with Change Course! instructors to share their writing, their classroom successes and problems, and the progress of classroom research studies that made up the final aspect of the program. The premises of Change Course! were three:

Effective teachers are writers and readers. When classroom teachers become serious writers who share their writing and their reading processes with their students, they model the activities they want students to do and better understand their students' struggles and achievements.

Effective teachers are professional educators. Becoming writers and readers isn't enough, however. To be truly effective, teachers must join the professional conversation about English teaching by becoming knowledgeable professionals, contributors, and researchers. In doing so, they discover what works, try new ideas, and determine sound teaching practices while learning to see their students in new ways.

All writing is creative. Instead of trying to distinguish between "expository" and "creative" writing, instruction in English should recognize that the activities and processes of creating and reading all forms of writing deserve equal attention at all levels of the curriculum.

The program participants, all successful, experienced teachers in traditional classrooms, moved to workshop teaching using these premises as a base from which to begin. This book presents the stories of nine of these teachers and their journeys.

Acknowledgments

This volume owes its existence to many people and to several institutions. In a very direct way, of course, the teachers whose essays comprise the core of the book deserve my thanks, since it is through their efforts, in the classroom and at the word processor, that the work presented here was accomplished. I have learned much from them about excellent teaching.

The individual who unquestionably casts the longest shadow here is Glenda L. Bissex, with whom I co-edited an earlier collection of classroom research essays. Whatever I have learned about classroom research—its procedures, its pedagogy, its promise—I have learned or borrowed from Glenda, a pioneer in the field.

I owe much to my colleagues in the Institute on Writing and Teaching at Wright State University, Nancy Mack and James Thomas of Wright State and Bob Fox of the Ohio Arts Council. Together, we developed the Institute and Change Course!, the foundations of this volume.

This brings me to the National Endowment for the Arts. The NEA's call for proposals for summer workshops to improve the teaching of creative writing in secondary schools led Nancy, James, Bob, and me to create Change Course!. The NEA's generous funding allowed us to implement the Change Course! program, which integrated current pedagogy in writing and reading with contemporary creative writing, and to strengthen the fruitful collaboration between Wright State's English Department and the Ohio Arts Council.

The Arts Council also deserves thanks, not just for Bob Fox's contributions as writer, administrator, and resident bluesman, but for its generous financial support over the past eight years, through which the Institute has been able to offer teachers the opportunity to work with nationally known poets, fiction writers, and essayists.

At Wright State University, the Institute and Change Course! have also been generously supported by Perry Moore, Provost; William Rickert, Acting Dean of the College of Liberal Arts; John Fleischauer, former Provost; Lillie Howard, Associate Provost; Henry Limouze, Chair of the Department of English; and the many other creative administrators and secretaries who have found ways to sustain an entity that doesn't match Wright State's typical course or program structure.

Jeanette Allen, the secretary for the English Department's writing programs, deserves special thanks for her help in scanning and preparing the manuscript of *Why Workshop?*, as well as for her unfailing cheerfulness, thoughtfulness, and competence at whatever she does.

Several reviewers and readers offered advice that has made this a much better book. Brenda Miller Power and Leila Christenbury, who reviewed my proposal for Stenhouse, gave me valuable suggestions that greatly influenced its shape. Once the manuscript was complete, my colleagues William E. Smith and Nancy Mack, and Change Course! teachers Mary Ann Pohlmeyer, Paula Lochotzki, and Lora Grillot Vallandingham, helped tremendously with their sensitive, careful readings.

Of course, this book would not exist had Philippa Stratton, Stenhouse's editor, not agreed that it fulfilled a real need. Thanks to her and to Linda Howe, who edited the copy, and Joyce C. Weston, who designed the book.

Finally, of course, I must thank my family. As my three sons, Ben, Mickey, and Jonathan, grow into young manhood, they fill me with pride and surprise me by eliciting surges of love as intense as those I felt when I first laid eyes on them. Barb, my wife, completes me.

CHAPTER 1

Why Workshop?

Coverage *(Knowing)* and Critical Thinking *(Doing)*

Most traditional curriculums talk about subjects in terms of content: grammar to be learned, literature to be read, types or modes of writing to be mastered. Teaching has followed that lead, focusing on what students need to be taught or "exposed to" (an interesting phrase) at each educational level. A good course, then, exposes students to the appropriate things, good teachers teach those things, and good students learn them. If a teacher "covers" the course content, she has done her job and done it well; students who can't "keep up" are at fault, as shown by their grades. Students who do keep up can show their mastery of the course content by doing well on standardized tests and by remembering (at least through the final exam) various terms of grammar and details from their reading. In this educational scheme, which is still very much with us, the primary emphasis is on *knowing:* knowledge is presented as an abstract, ill-defined end in itself.

At the same time, though, there has always been another way of seeing education, even in traditional, content-centered classrooms and curriculums, a way based on *doing.* To understand the content in a piece of literature, students have to know how to read; to master ways of writing, they have to know how to write; to show mastery of grammar, they have to use grammar correctly in their writing and in their speech. Over the last quarter-century, more and more educational experts and teachers have come to see the primacy of *process.* They reason that in a world in which

1

specific knowledge changes rapidly, students need to learn *how* to learn. Workshop teaching begins with this precept.

"Traditional" and "Workshop" Teaching

The terms "traditional" and "workshop" refer not only to specific practices but also to basic philosophies of teaching. Since the implementation of those philosophies varies greatly from teacher to teacher and from classroom to classroom, the meaning of "traditional" and "workshop" teaching varies. Yet however individuals construe them, the two methods share identifiable primary characteristics:

Traditional	**Workshop**
The teacher (or school or state) designs and implements the curriculum.	Teacher and students negotiate curriculum, both individually and in groups (within mandated constraints).
Students practice skills and memorize facts.	Students actively construct concepts and meanings.
Content is broken down into discrete, sequential units.	Content is presented whole, in meaningful contexts.
Products (finished pieces of writing, answers on tests) are of primary importance.	Processes (prewriting, composing multiple drafts; exploring how answers were arrived at; self-evaluation) are valued as much as the products themselves.
Avoiding mistakes is important.	Taking risks is valued as a sign of learning.
Performance on tests is valued highly.	Students are assessed by their performance on meaningful tasks, often through portfolios of their work.
Teachers do the evaluating and grading.	Students learn to assess their own learning and progress.
Learning is expected to be uniform. Expectations are the same for all students, so many students "fail."	Learning is expected to be individual and unique. Evaluation is oriented toward success.

(adapted from Weaver 15)

Obviously, a classroom where learning is based on workshops is very different from a traditional classroom. In a workshop class, students may study thematic units that combine various genres and activities instead of doing units of poetry, grammar, or essays. Within those thematic units, they can often choose their own reading and writing assignments, either from lists of suggestions or through negotiation with the teacher. They take class time to explore writing through various prewriting or invention activities and then write several drafts, asking both the teacher and their fellow students for their responses along the way. Rather than doing things they know they can already do and playing it safe, students in workshop classes are encouraged to try new activities, to take risks, to stretch themselves.

This encouragement comes in part from changes in how they are assessed: instead of scores on "objective" tests and grades on individual pieces of writing assigned by the teacher, students may compile a portfolio collection containing several pieces of their writing, entries from their reading journal, and other sorts of evidence to show that they have worked, strived, and learned. Students evaluate the contents of their own portfolio to learn to see their own strengths and weaknesses and address them, instead of relying on the teacher to tell them what they did well or badly. Throughout the year, students work at their own pace within the framework and rhythm of the class. They experience success at the same time that academic standards are upheld—or even raised.

Of course, these characterizations are unlikely to be found in a "pure" form in any one classroom. Classrooms typically reflect teachers' experience, their personalities, and their sense of what works for their students. Still, each class, each curriculum is likely to be skewed toward one philosophy or another, due in part to the teacher's training, but more particularly to the context within which the teacher and the class work.

And many factors influence that context. The existing curriculum, which may be mandated by the school, the district, or the state, is probably traditional. Fellow teachers, parents, and community members may believe that the traditional way they were educated is the way children *should* be educated. And the textbooks in the classroom's closets—the literature anthologies with questions at the end of each selection, the handbooks, the vocabulary workbooks—all promote a vision of the traditional content-centered education to be delivered in that classroom. At the same time, however, professional journals, teacher-education programs, and inservice and summer workshops promote activity-based teaching, workshop teaching, *process* teaching. Yet under even the best of circumstances, teachers have limited freedom to alter their teaching, and a sense of professional responsibility makes many hesitant to try new things. In this situation, is it any wonder that teachers feel unsure of themselves and find making changes in their teaching difficult, even acts of courage?

Basic Skills and Experiential Learning

Successful teaching requires organization: lesson plans must be clear, their scope and sequence outlined, classroom rules carefully articulated, and time managed if teachers are to survive five or six periods of teaching daily, three or four preparations, and 150 teenagers. For traditional teachers, moving to workshop teaching can be difficult because traditional teaching is *tidy*. In many traditional curriculums, content is broken down into small pieces and doled out to students one digestible bit at a time. Activities such as writing are recast as an accumulation of discrete skills, which can be further divided: first, students learn about simple sentences, then add some phrases, move to clauses, then paragraphs, then five paragraph themes, and so on. Many secondary curriculums follow this atomized, sequential view of how written language is best learned.

Workshop teaching, by contrast, is messy. Students talk together, work together, perhaps even sit on the floor (!); and twenty-five students may be reading twenty-five different books or working on individualized and very different writing projects all at once. But the workshop teacher sees messiness as a sign that learning—defined not as mastery of discrete skills but as integrated, meaningful use of language in reading and writing, speaking and listening—is going on. In this view, students learn not piece by piece, little by little, in carefully isolated bits; they learn by engaging in activities that have meaning for them. Students acquire the language skills they need in the context of communicating with others.

Such a classroom sounds attractive to many teachers, but its apparent messiness can cause them to think twice. Teachers whose classes are orderly, whose lesson plans are carefully worked out from day one to the end of the school year, might reasonably ask of workshop classrooms, "Who's in control here?"

Control and Choice

Who's in control? Good question. A traditional teacher in a traditional classroom creates conditions that leave no doubt in anyone's mind about who is in control, and one of the basic lessons new teachers need to learn is how to achieve and maintain that control. When I first started teaching, I was assigned to an eighth grade class in a suburban middle school. It was a school out of control. Every time I looked out my first-floor classroom windows, I could see papers, books, and—once—a desk, flying out the second-floor windows. Even the principal had no authority with the students, who openly ignored him. I spent my time there simply trying to keep the students in their seats and in the classroom. We struggled through novels and plays, paragraphs and themes, as I pursued the elusive goal of a quiet, smoothly running classroom where students worked quietly at their seats or listened attentively to my sensitive and brilliant lectures. The reality was more akin to a large animal caretaker: keep them occupied and never turn your back.

When I moved to university teaching, I started out as a basic writing teacher. To my surprise I found that control problems didn't stop once students got their high school diplomas. I had students who brought to college the same behavior and attitudes that had made them less-than-stellar high school students, sometimes intensified by their new freedom and their fear that they wouldn't make it in college. Instead of trying to squelch them, I adopted a workshop approach and behavior problems—talking when I was lecturing, moving around the room during class, not doing the activity I had planned—went away. I didn't lose control, I simply exchanged one form of control for another. Still, it was difficult. I'd gotten it into my head that there is one proper role for teachers and one proper role for students, so that moving to a different set of roles was not only hard, it was scary.

The Comfort of Stasis

Advocates for change often blame teachers. In a world where they are constantly under attack, many teachers understandably despair of sorting out the just from the unjust criticism and hunker down until the latest "crisis" abates. The result, however, is that schools tend toward stasis; that stasis is usually firmly traditional—and ultimately unfair to students. Joan Estes Barickman, a veteran high school history and English teacher, describes a type of teacher common to many schools:

> *Mr. Jenkins is one of the most popular teachers I know, particularly with "average" and "below-average" students. He's a fill-in-the-blank man. Basically, all that his students do is read short passages from his history textbook and fill in the blanks at the end of each section. His multiple choice tests come from the publisher. His class is popular because he*

> *meets many of the students' needs. He gives them stability*
> *and predictability; their goals, responsibilities, and achieve-*
> *ments are quite clear. (1992, 41)*

Many of the students who emerge from this experience of education are like Barickman's Andy:

> *Andy comes to school already knowing the "truths" of his*
> *culture and family. He doesn't want to question values or*
> *methods. He's afraid of ambiguity and new ideas. He just*
> *wants to avoid being wrong. . . . Andy thinks school learning*
> *is attending classes . . . and "doing" schoolwork. . . . If he does*
> *that, he assumes he's learning. His reading is decoding, not*
> *comprehending; his writing is copying straight out of his*
> *head or the book, not composing. He memorizes by looking*
> *at his book; he takes tests by what he remembers. (10-11)*

Teacher and student participate in school in ways that are both familiar and accepted. Mr. Jenkins's classroom is safe and predictable, his lesson plans detailed and complete. The better students know what to do to succeed in his class, though asking them to take chances that might jeopardize their high grades—or relieve their boredom—is asking for trouble. The Andys, on the other hand, have a harder time. Although they do what they think is expected of them, they are likely to fail. Barickman says, "We owe Andy. We make him go to school. Then we make him feel stupid" (14). We also owe the better students. We make them go to school, too, and we make them feel smart, but often that smartness comes at a high price: timidity at approaching new or difficult tasks and a preoccupation with grades as the sole goal of education. The better students, the Andys, and the ones in between are why teachers begin to move away from traditional teaching and toward workshop.

So Why Workshop?

Simply stated, workshop teaching balances students' need to be challenged with their need to progress at their own individual pace. In the classrooms described in this volume, some students read *Macbeth* while others in the same class tackle *To Kill a Mockingbird* or build their skills and confidence with picture books. Some students write complex essays, others write short stories, and still others write letters. All are progressing, all are being challenged, but no one is being ignored or left out. Mr. Jenkins's class ignores students who are ready to think about the subject. The classroom Sherri S. Hall abandoned (See Chapter 2) ignored the less able students. Workshop teaching allows teachers to pitch their teaching to everyone in the room, smart or not, learning-disabled or not, honors or vocational.

Workshop teaching also moves students more directly toward the ultimate goal of schooling, which is to produce thoughtful citizens of a democracy. "Up until now, our major emphasis in school has been wrong: we have focused on acquisition of knowledge, rather than use; on breadth of data, rather than depth of personal understanding; and on information alone, rather than information, skills, and attitudes together" (Barickman 1992, 57). Traditional teaching, with its emphasis on information and a classroom structure that focuses on the teacher as authority and authoritarian, is a poor way to give students a sense of what it takes to be a capable citizen "in the adult world where the real tests are what you can do" (Barickman 1992, 57)—and where good citizens question those in authority. Workshop asks students to work together, despite differences in ability; to set goals and attempt to meet them; to engage in real communication with real audiences; to take responsibility for their work; to complete meaningful tasks and assess them according to criteria developed collaboratively. Workshop breaks down the division between school work (writing done in response to prompts, assigned reading, tests) and adult work (writing done in response to various needs, self-chosen reading, demonstrations of competence). Workshop teaching is, ultimately, more ethical teaching because students at all levels learn to be successful adults and citizens.

Changing Course

Why Workshop? is arranged in three sections. The first, "'I'm a Good Teacher, But . . .': Deciding What to Keep and What to Change," begins with a discussion of some of the reasons why change is difficult and some of the ways it can be made easier. Then Sherri S. Hall describes the development of her perfect, traditional classroom, "Sherriland," and why she abandoned it in favor of workshop teaching, changing her view of herself as a teacher in the process. What motivated Merikay Roth Larrabee, a teacher of eleventh and twelfth graders, though, was the change she made in herself when she took the advice of workshop teaching advocates and became a writer. Her essay shows how becoming a writer, rather than simply remaining a reader of the writing of others, forced significant changes in her classroom.

Part 2, "'What Do I Do on Monday (and Tuesday, Wednesday, Thursday, and Friday?)': Experimenting with Workshop Teaching," moves from *why* to *how:* how did successful traditional teachers implement workshop teaching in their classrooms? Paula Lochotzki, a teacher in a girls' parochial high school, conceives of her moves as exchanges: replacing certain practices with others that would more completely meet her goals. Cheryl H. Almeda, who teaches in an urban high school, describes how she learned to exploit her students' concern for their peers' opinions to their benefit as writers by encouraging them to write and publish for one another. Debra Ciambro Grisso spent most of a year struggling to design reading response assignments that would elicit thoughtful, interesting writing from her middle school students; she recounts her successes and her failures—but also her persistence in believing that she could make this facet of workshop teaching work for her students. Creating a classroom atmosphere in which eighth graders could successfully conduct peer conferences is the focus of Richard D. Hughes's essay. Debra's and Ric's chapters exemplify the extent to which change in classrooms is the result of trial and error, tinkering, adjusting, learning from mistakes as from successes.

As most teachers know, in the classroom all is never roses, for there are always students who do not cooperate, who try to become invisible, who exert themselves to offend. Part 3, "'What About the Kid Who . . .?': Workshop Teaching and 'Difficult' Students," explores ways in which workshop teaching can engage and bring into the academic conversation students who are too often outside it. Mary Anne Anderson's profile of Frank, a troubled middle school student, offers insights into how and to what extent such students can be reached through workshop teaching. The vocational students who are the focus of Suzanne E. Theisen's essay have, by and large, been abandoned by regular schooling and left to graduate vocationally skilled but semiliterate at best. Suzanne's essay shows that such low expectations may reflect popular prejudice, not reality. And Theresa L. McClain's examination of the progress of three "heavy metal" adolescents through tenth grade English shows the importance of peers and their potential effect on one another in a nurturing academic setting.

Throughout, these nine teachers describe their classrooms, their students, their methods, their lessons and their ways of implementing them to offer a kaleidoscopic view of how workshop teaching operates in various middle school and high school English classrooms. To illustrate the nitty-gritty of making workshop teaching work, Stephanie Walter Corcoran, a middle school teacher who has been a workshop teacher over her entire career, offers a sampler of the letters, forms, checksheets, and assessment tools she uses in her classroom (see the appendix). These documents are excellent starting points for teachers wishing to develop their own organizational tools.

Taken together, these essays provide a useful window on the process of change. Unlike much teacher-oriented literature, they do not sidestep the sloppy business of moving from one teaching method to another, from one self-image to another, or the courage, thought, and tenacity that such movement entails. Changing course is indeed difficult, but these teachers clearly show that the benefits are worth the journey.

"I'm a Good Teacher, But . . .": Deciding What to Keep and What to Change

Secondary Teachers Caught in the Middle

The decision to move from one way of teaching to another can produce anxious questions: Will students learn what I think they need to learn? Will they learn what the teacher next year expects them to learn? Will they do well on proficiency tests, the SAT, the ACT? Will I "lose" some, and if so, which ones? If they don't read [fill in the blank: Shakespeare, Keats, *To Kill a Mockingbird*] now, when will they? If they don't write a research paper, how will they learn those skills?

These are important questions not to be brushed aside as unimportant or evidence of insufficient professional development. The answers will determine whether or not any given teacher will change what he or she does, so they deserve serious consideration. Some teachers find that their students learn best through a choice-driven curriculum and put their faith in the workshop to eventually round out students' educational experience. Others establish guidelines—"Read one Shakespeare play from this list during the year"; "Include at least one outside source in each essay this term"—to ensure that students will get what they need. Still others set aside time for whole-class activities, including reading certain works as a class and discussing them together. The point is, moving from traditional teaching to workshop teaching can seem drastic, yet one need not have a conversion experience (though they often happen, sooner or later). I've met lots of True Believers in whole language and workshop teaching; I've met even more teachers who are interested, and see the benefits, but are leery of dropping everything familiar and starting anew. This is a reasonable and natural response to the prospect of change.

Understanding Change and Its Difficulties

Seven Principles of Change

Given all the difficulties facing secondary teachers who wish to change their methods, it's little wonder that many end up reverting to their previous ways. And what's true of teachers is true of people in general and of organizations, including schools. Finding ways to understand the dynamics of change is crucial to success. One perspective comes from organizational development, a multidisciplinary field that "consists of planned efforts to help persons work and live together more effectively, over time, in their organizations" (Hanson and Lubin 1989, 16). Organizations include all the structured social situations in which people find themselves: schools, businesses, even families. Walter Sikes, a psychologist who studies change, has identified seven principles that help make sense of reactions to change (1989, 179), and each of these principles has clear implications for teachers and schools.

1. *You must understand something thoroughly before you try to change it.* This principle is at work when, for example, teachers feel pressured to adopt a new method yet remain unsure about how to implement it or unclear about why it's superior to their current method. In my work with portfolio assessment, I have encountered teachers who say they have "tried portfolios" but found that "they didn't work." When I ask them to describe what they did, I learn that they may have asked students to keep their papers in a folder and even to choose their best pieces for a showcase portfolio. But the teachers still mark every error in red pen and grade each paper, while wondering why students don't revise (except to fix what was pointed out to them) and seem unable to assess their own writing. Despite their good intentions and willingness to innovate, they had missed a central point of portfolio grading: to avoid evaluating pieces of writing in isolation. To make change happen—and make it stick—you have to know what you're doing and why.

2. *You cannot change just one element of a system.* [*Systems resist change.*] Classrooms, like schools, corporations, and families, are amazingly complex systems. Changing one aspect can often lead to unforeseen changes in other parts of the system, which will resist those changes. "Sys-

tems [work systems, school systems, classroom systems, family systems, interpersonal systems] are generally biased against change," Sikes notes. "Individuals wishing to change their roles or behavior tend to encounter much pressure from the system to remain as they are, no matter how unsatisfactory this is" (181).

Traditional teachers pressure innovators to abandon new ways, knowing that successful innovations will force them to change in turn. If middle school teachers abandon the formal teaching of grammar in favor of teaching grammar in the context of students' writing, for instance, high school teachers must either abandon their expectation that students will know grammatical terms or teach grammar themselves. One teacher working alone may be made to feel that she is harming her students by failing to prepare them for the classroom they'll go into the following year, and so abandon a new curriculum. This is common among novice teachers, who quickly learn that the lessons they learned in their college methods courses do not fit "the way we do things here."

3. *People resist anything they feel is punishment.* As Sikes observes, "At a minimum, change makes one exert additional energy, either in making the change oneself or adapting to it. [Also, trying] something new means testing the limits of one's competence, which is scary" (182). In other words, one's self-worth is intimately tied to changing, so *not* changing is safer. Also, change creates pressure: Where do you turn for help or assurance? What if you fail? What if your students don't learn? Much of the time we focus only on the results of change efforts, and since not all efforts work out, we stand a good chance of "failing." Never mind what we learned from the attempt. If it doesn't work, and work the first time, we feel bad and think we look bad in the eyes of others.

4. *People are reluctant to endure discomfort even for the sake of possible gains.* Sikes notes that "we are reluctant to go beyond the limits of our known, tested abilities" (183), and our reluctance grows when what we have to gain from changing is uncertain. Moving from a comfortable style of teaching is hard, not least because we may not know for several months or longer whether or not what we're doing is successful. And as teachers, we don't want to harm our students by doing something that may not work, even if the odds are good that their learning will improve.

5. *Change always generates stress.* "All change, pleasant or unpleasant, causes stress" (184). Routines are comforting; ruts have their purposes. In a stressful world, maintaining an area in which we control what's going on and can predict what will happen each day can be psychologically important. Giving up that "safe" area is inherently stressful. When faced with the

prospect of change, how many teachers purposely retreat behind the closed doors of their classrooms and into their carefully constructed lesson plans, where they feel comfortable, safe, and competent?

6. *Participation in setting goals and devising strategies reduces resistance to change.* If your principal, your state legislature, or an author in *English Journal* tells you to change, you're likely to resist. Why? Not only for the reasons given above, but also because your control over your teaching is being taken away from you. If, however, you have some say in what to change and how to change (even if not changing isn't an option), you're likely to feel better about those changes and be more likely to implement them.

7. *Behavioral change comes in small steps.* As the people who "tried" portfolios but found that they "didn't work" demonstrate, trying to change some parts of one's teaching while leaving other parts alone can lead to failure; but trying to change everything all at once can also lead to failure. Teachers I've known who "tried" a whole new way of teaching but rejected it as "not working" jumped in without knowing enough about what they were doing to anticipate and deal with unforeseen problems, or didn't have the support they needed from fellow teachers, administrators, or professional sources.

Others have adopted whole new curriculums and survived, partly because they learned a lot about those curriculums, partly because they designed and adapted them for their own situations, and partly because they received support from one another and from professional sources. Still other teachers who have moved more slowly have succeeded by adopting what Sikes identifies as "experiments that move them toward a goal" (185), in other words, not random insertions of new material into a curriculum, but carefully designed changes that can be integrated into existing teaching while preserving the premises and the spirit of the desired change.

Lurking behind these statements is an eighth one that seems of particular importance to teachers: *Change alters our control of our situation.* Almost every essay in this book discusses change in the context of control: who controls the curriculum, who decides what students read or write, who assesses whom. In very real ways, to change is to lose control, or to face periods of adjustment. When we move to workshop teaching, we alter the ways we control students' activities in our classroom; when we write and share our writing with our students, we show vulnerability; when we announce to colleagues, administrators, and parents that we are trying something new, we risk criticism. Part of the comfort of not changing derives from our feeling that we have achieved control over our situation. To change we must feel that the results are worth the risk.

Changing One's Curriculum, Changing One's Self

Making sense of change and how we react to it is one thing; actually changing is another. This book is composed of essays by teachers who changed their curriculums, their sense of who they are as teachers, and sometimes their sense of who they are, period. These changes didn't come easily; they demanded commitment and self-motivation, and progress was often uneven. Generally, however, what sustained these teachers as they worked out their new teaching styles, new curriculums, and new identities, was their growing sense of the rightness of their actions. As they struggled, they saw that their students learned more, and they felt better about their teaching and themselves.

This sense of well-being is the focus of the two initial essays by Sherri S. Hall and Merikay Roth Larrabee. Both teachers demonstrate the truth of Sikes's seven principles of change, although in different ways. Hall discovered that she needed to overcome considerable stress in order to initiate successful changes and did so by asserting her ultimate control over her classroom rather than by trying to adopt someone else's ideas. Larrabee, on the other hand, found that she understood writers only when she started writing and got past her sense that writing can be punishing or even dangerous. For both, workshop teaching became possible once they had dealt with curricular and emotional matters. What unites their essays is their recognition that they did not change successfully until they felt an internal, personal need to do so. They benefited from help and support, but ultimately what spurred them on was not a mandate from above or pressure from without. Sherri felt a need to avoid stagnation, Merikay a need to become a better workshop teacher.

CHAPTER 2

Adventures in Sherriland

Sherri S. Hall

> *If you love whole language, have never taught language any other way, are appalled that there are those who still teach the "other" way, this is not about you or for you. If you are one of those who still teach the "other" way, however, and are interested in change but afraid, be brave. Welcome to Sherriland.*

Where Was I and How in the World Did I Ever Get Here?

Teachers know that teaching is an autonomous activity. Much of what we do, we do in isolation. We all go to our rooms and shut our doors. We become very protective of what we do and how we do it. Administrators tend to reinforce this isolation, often as a means of dividing and conquering. The autonomy can be a blessing, the isolation, a curse. I realized after my first disastrous year of teaching that I needed to create my own space. The isolation was part of my problem and the autonomy was part of my solution.

Teachers create learning environments for students all the time. I needed to create one that my students and I could grow in. I had discipline problems galore my first year. I could make, and have made, the entire list of excuses—class size, bad kids, bad room, inadequate materials. But I realized that I was the source of the problem. Even after thirteen successful years of teaching, that's hard to admit. But it was me. I wasn't prepared to teach. My classes were out of control. I hadn't thought through what I

16

wanted or needed to do. And I certainly hadn't thought through *how* I would do it.

During the summer following my first year of teaching I spent a lot of time thinking. I was fortunate enough to be rehired and was to have a new classroom. I felt I could start over but I knew it would be difficult. I had allowed dangerous precedents that would need to be changed.

I set out to create what ultimately became "Sherriland." I organized and scheduled and read and created. Before the school year started, I put up posters, created bulletin board displays, wrote out my pupil performance objectives, and placed "good" books on the shelves. I knew where we would be at any given point in the year. I would reign over this class. It would be mine.

It worked. At least parts of it worked. The discipline was better. My students didn't have time to breathe, let alone get into trouble. Students were working hard to do well. I took pride in the fact that I gave so few A's and wrote so many deficiency reports.

As for the posters and the books, well, the posters looked nice, but so did the books. I'm not sure a single student touched a book except a textbook all year. Sometimes I'd try to guide one to a particular book, but there was never any time to read: we had textbooks to get through. I loved telling students at the beginning of the year that we would cover everything in both the grammar and the literature texts. (The shock on their faces!) And we did. I had decided not to teach to the median but to the higher-level learner. Gifted kids were challenged in my class; for many it was the only class in which they really had to work. Average kids had to work hard just to be average. And the lower levels? There were a lot of Special Ed. placements; these students couldn't keep up and everyone knew it.

I thought, "This is great. I'm really teaching here." I believed that good teachers covered the material (the textbook), kept students busy, and had few discipline problems. That, after all, was what every teaching evaluation I had ever seen considered important. And that's certainly the way it was in my classroom.

I was, and still am, a compulsive organizer. I devised lesson plans and activities files for each of my classes. At the end of each unit I would reflect not on what worked or didn't but on where I needed more stuff to keep my students busy. And I added more stuff.

I was in charge. It was Sherriland—the imaginary place I had created in my classroom, where everything was the way I wanted it to be. I know that this style of teaching is teacher-centered. And I know that there are thousands of teachers like me in classrooms everywhere. I made all the decisions: who did *what, when, where,* and *how.* After all, I had "the big desk." But I rarely thought about *why.*

Slowly I came to the question I had avoided for so long. I had organized and filled fifty-seven-minute periods with materials: worksheets, handouts, projects, vocabulary exercises, outside reading, quizzes, and tests. But when I had finally filled in all the blank blocks of time, what more was I to do? I had organized the curriculum, written the lecture notes, filled in the time lines. It occurred to me that anyone could come in and teach my class as well as I did. And if that were the case, I thought, what now?

It troubled me. I thought, "This can't be it! Have I done everything I need to do to teach for the remaining fifteen-plus years of my career?! Now I just coast?"

It was a very uncomfortable time. I was proud to be a teacher, and I believed I was a good teacher. I believed students really learned in my classroom, and I didn't want the learning to stop, for them or for me. It was hard to realize that I wasn't needed. I'd produced a teacher-centered curriculum where the teacher wasn't really needed. I had written an impersonal textbook: any teacher would do. And that hurt my ego.

So I did what most of us who love language do when we face a crisis or a challenge: I turned to books. I asked a lot of questions, and I didn't always like the answers. Often the answers only led to more questions.

As teachers we encounter what is almost an institutionalized lack of respect. Parents and society as a whole may tell us we are doing a fine job, but they also say that the schools are failing. "In the United States the tendency is to treat and train teachers more like recovering alcoholics: subjecting them to step-by-step programs of effective instruction or conflict management or professional growth in ways which make them overly dependent on pseudoscientific expertise developed and imposed by others" (Hargreaves 1994, xiv).

My training made me believe I couldn't have the answers because I didn't have the right to find the answers. Although I have an M.A. in English with an emphasis in rhetoric and composition, I still didn't feel I had the authority to say no to "traditional" textbook approaches. I had no legitimacy, and I realized that the way I was teaching only perpetuated that.

I read Nancie Atwell and wondered where she got the perfect kids. I read Donald Graves and thought about how distant my real-world classroom was from his. I began to think that the education hierarchy was right: Maybe I couldn't know the answers. Maybe I didn't have the authority to say no.

And then I got angry.

Who are "they," I thought, to tell me what is right for my students? They have never met my kids. They don't know what is happening in my classroom. What right do they have to set me up to feel inadequate?

I began reading about change and professional development in education. Most of what I read was encouraging, but I wondered why the people who design in-services didn't read this stuff. In his book *Changing Teachers, Changing Times,* Andy Hargreaves discusses the basic changes needed in school structures if schools are to meet the needs of a post-industrial society: "We are beginning to recognize that, for teachers, what goes on inside the classroom is closely related to what goes on outside it. The quality, range and flexibility of teachers' classroom work is closely tied up with their professional growth—the way that they develop as people and as professionals" (1994, ix). I knew that if I wanted to change my classroom, I had to be willing to change myself.

I had to give up the idea that I knew it all. I didn't, and teaching a gifted group had helped me to admit it. (These kids will eat you alive if you try to bluff them.) So, I was comfortable with not being the "great giver" of knowledge. Not so comfortable was not being in control: How much authority do I abdicate? How much do I retain? The questions haunted me.

When I began learning about whole language, I felt apologetic about "Sherriland." Now I've come to realize that there is no reason to apologize. My classroom can be anything I want it to be, just as it always has been; but now I want it to be workshop-based, more student-centered. A critical moment came when I finally realized that these elements—workshop and portfolios—could be what I *wanted* them to be, what my students *needed* them to be. In order to "do workshop" I didn't have to be exactly like Atwell or Rief or Giacobbe. I could still be "Queen Sherri" and design a workshop that worked for me and my kids.

For instance, I have trouble believing that my students could peer-conference and get just as much out of the experience as they could in conferring with me. There are a few seventh and eighth graders who can confer with their peers and cover the material as well as I do, but most of them can't. At least not yet. It's unrealistic to believe that they can. They still need me.

And I need them. I need my students to remind me why I no longer teach from the textbook. I need them to keep me fresh. I need to know that something is happening out there. It's a lot messier in "Sherriland," but it's also a lot more exciting.

For one thing, I learn things from my junior high students that I really don't want to know—personal things, private things. But now I have the time and an avenue for pursuing these issues in private conferences if need be. As a result, I feel that I know my students better. I certainly don't like them all. Some of them are pains. And they don't all succeed, but I'm used to that. When I taught the other way, I didn't like them all either, and a lot more didn't succeed. I know that each year I will continue to nip and tuck and add and subtract to accommodate the changes students need.

Finding a support group of other teachers was an important aspect of my success. During my first year of workshop teaching there were times when I believed I wouldn't make it. I felt sure I was headed for burnout. I needed to know that workshop works. And that I was not alone. I needed to hear that others were having the same, or worse, problems that I was. And I needed to hear suggestions for improvement. Change takes an enormous amount of personal and professional commitment. For me, it was important to be with people who were unwilling to let me fail. It was also important that I had made a public commitment. Otherwise, I would have given up by October. After all, I had spent eleven years learning how to teach the "other" way. It was very safe, and parts of it were wonderful. But even though workshop isn't the perfect answer to all students' problems, it is far better than the "other" way. I just needed the time to find out how to make it work for me.

I try to remember that I can't expect something to work for students if it doesn't work for me. According to Bratcher and Stroble, "lasting change in the teaching of writing depends on the teacher's level of comfort and skills" (1994, 72). That is not to say that I believe all my students must be like me. Some respond to things I don't. The individual differences are what makes this job a tough one, but a good one.

I need to believe I can give to students and they can give back. What makes it all work is the give and take. Reading and writing are life skills that have an important influence on who these students are and what they become. Try to convince me that a corporate CEO has that kind of responsibility. As a teacher I will be blasted from all sides as overpaid, underworked, and incompetent, but not one of my detractors will trade places with me for a week. I know the classroom is where I belong. I may have other "crises" of faith, but that self-knowledge is important.

As educators, we are often told what to teach and even how to teach. (In the state of Ohio, for example, English teachers work under the "threat" of a ninth-grade proficiency test.) We often work under less than ideal conditions—interruptions, cancellations, student disruptions, overly large classes. In many respects, it's a miracle that anything of value is accomplished. And yet I know that for the majority of my students, great things are happening. Real learning is taking place, and this miracle is happening in classrooms all over this country.

At the end of my first year as a workshop teacher, I handed out end-of-year evaluations to my students as usual. They could fill these out anonymously, but many gave their names. Then, although I was a bit hesitant, I decided to send one to their parents. I was anxious, but I need not have been. The students' responses were gratifying. "I do feel I've changed. I never realized how much I liked reading and writing," one eighth grader wrote. Another said, "The class was hard, but it changed me into a reader and a writer." (My heart soared as I read that one!) A seventh grader wrote, "I never knew English could be that much fun!"

Their parents were also positive. "This program encouraged the students to think and really use their imaginations." "Jayson only read when he absolutely had to before, now he actually takes a book to bed every night. This is truly amazing." And finally, one parent, who wrote two pages, summed up what many parents had expressed: "I think this has been a very positive experience for the students. I would like to see this program incorporated into a standard curriculum so that the students wouldn't feel so insecure about what they are learning. They were so used to the standard methods of learning that they were afraid that they had missed something this year. I think they were wrong and am pleased they had a chance to learn in a different way." Research supports what I am doing, but these evaluations were far more powerful.

I need to know that I have real power. Control isn't power. Power is creating an arena where learning can take place and letting it happen. My classroom is still Sherriland. It is still the environment I create for my students and I am still "Queen Sherri." But now we're a constitutional monarchy—the power is shared.

CHAPTER 3

Viewing Myself as a Writer: The Roots of True Authority in the Writing Classroom

Merikay Roth Larrabee

Myself

When I was fifteen, I wrote a poem filled with teenage angst. I wrote my next poem at fifty-three in a summer workshop called "The Experience of Writing." In the thirty-eight years between my two poems, I wrote countless papers for undergraduate and graduate classes and "taught" writing to hundreds of students. I viewed myself as an arbiter of good writing, but I never viewed myself as a writer. Like my colleagues, I assigned topics and required final drafts, complete with outlines, to be turned in each Friday. I spent hours with my red pen correcting mechanical and organizational errors and writing lengthy comments designed to help my students improve their writing, only to be disappointed when they looked at the grade and ignored my commentary.

Dissatisfied with the results of classroom writing strategies, I attended workshops and read articles, eventually finding Nancie Atwell and Donald Graves. Convinced that the writing workshop offered the solution I'd been seeking, I typed forms, organized my classroom, and announced to my classes that henceforth we would be a writing workshop. After two months, however, I was ready to give up. The idea of student choice and the minilessons on problem areas worked well, but on the whole, the workshop was floundering. A few students had completed several written pieces, but the majority either were not writing at all or were going from draft to draft just to meet the minimum requirements. Accustomed only to judging the end product, I was not sure how to guide their efforts.

Not wanting to surrender, I returned to Atwell and Graves for answers. The message that I had successfully ignored during my first reading of their books came through loud and clear: teachers of writing must be writers. When the opportunity came along to be a part of "The Experience of Writing," I resolved to see if my reading of Graves and Atwell were correct—and signed up for the poetry section.

It's enough to make one believe in the Muses or a benevolent fate: by a lucky chance I was assigned to Herbert Woodward Martin's poetry group. Several class members talked about their years of writing poetry and the problems that poets encounter. Herb, with his gentle, accepting manner, listened to all the comments and then spoke about his own experiences, showed us his writer's notebook, and talked about the continuing struggle to find ideas and time to write.

Only in retrospect did I realize how important the nonintimidating atmosphere he established was to the fledgling writers in the group. The class could so easily have become merely a dialogue between the published and the experienced, leaving the rest of us out of the loop and feeling even more inferior. Herb, however, enabled the beginners to feel comfortable.

Taking it a step farther, he initially assigned formula poems, challenging the experienced writers in the group to work within a framework and giving us beginners parameters within which we could achieve some degree of success. Of course, he spoke of these formulas or "recipes" as good ways to ease into poetry. He viewed them as a version of five-finger piano exercises: a certain amount of formulated practice is beneficial, because it allows players to gain skills they will be able to use automatically later.

When we arrived in the classroom with our "recipe" poems, he encouraged us to read them aloud, found something positive to say about each effort, and invited the rest of us to add positive comments. I survived the first assignment, and I was accepting Herb's view of what a poet (writer) needs to do—I kept my writer's notebook in my purse and collected placemats from Wendy's and the local Chinese restaurant as possible sources for writing ideas.

Herb opened one session by saying that he'd written a poem that morning, and though it was still in progress, that he'd like to read it to us. Flattered, we listened to his draft and understood his message: The teacher needs to share his or her own writing process, and every piece of writing is "in progress" and will be changed many times before it's "published" and even after. Nothing is written in stone. What a simple and yet liberating idea that was! And how much I needed the assurance that experimenting and changing were allowed, even encouraged.

Once the poetry workshop concluded, I continued sharing writing with an ongoing writing group. My group was clearly mystified by my poem entitled "Five-Finger Exercise #5, Musing on the Campus Want-ads":

> I'd like to go to the Mountain Top Bookstore
> (And Self-development Center).
> Are they on the pinnacle of success
> Or on the height of inspiration?
>
> Is there a loftier calling at
> Galaxy 10: Self-help, Metaphysics, Books?
>
> To take a step beyond, consult
> Mister Silver M. Shadow for readings in
> Tarot, Palm, I Ching.
>
> I record my blues at Refraze Recording Studios,
> Selling them back to Laid Back Records (new & used).
>
> If I can't find the keys to my existence
> (or the improvement thereof), I can find the keys
> to the ACE, PSAT, SAT, GMAT, GRE, LSAT, MCAT, NCLEX,
> USMLE, TOEFL at Kaplan:
> The answer to the test question.
> On a need to know basis only,
> ASAP, of course.
>
> Please refer any lingering creases or crimps to
> Not a Wrinkle Ironing Service
> or to Marybeth: Holistic Bodyworker!
>
> The perfect end to a perfect day . . .

Being thoroughly nice people, they gently probed my motives and looked for hidden meanings. Finally someone dared to ask, "What was all that stuff about want-ads? Was it supposed to make sense?" I explained that, following one of Herb's suggestions, I was having fun playing with some of the words and phrases I had found in the want-ads, trying to make a poem from them. I wasn't ready to risk anything more—to put my inner self on the line—and this playing allowed me to see words and language in a new way that I found refreshing and liberating. It stretched existing ideas into a new framework and exposed endless opportunities. A writing group responds to questions about the draft, offers suggestions for problem areas, celebrates the best moments, and points out the incomprehensible. The group allows each writer to write within his or her comfort zone while encouraging experimentation.

Being part of a writing group gave me an inside view of the advantages for both fledgling and experienced writers. Once the school year began, I discovered that I depended on the group to force me to write and to respond intelligently to my work. At first I relished all the positive comments because they muzzled the little beast in my brain which insists that I really can't write anything worth reading.

However, as I gained some degree of confidence, and expressed more of myself in my writing, my needs shifted subtly. While I still needed group members—my readers—to find the small gem in a paragraph of undistinguished words, I also needed them to tell me what didn't work and to speculate on why it didn't. Communicating effectively with any reader became an important part of my agenda, and I wanted criticism from other writers, especially those whose opinions I respected, that would help me do just that. Surprisingly, even the more experienced writers seemed to look to the group for the same things.

Another important aspect of our writing group was the informal publishing of our pieces each month in a photocopied booklet. I looked forward to receiving each booklet and eagerly read each piece, including those I had already heard during a group session. Seeing my own work in print conferred a status upon it that a rough draft could not.

In her book *Radical Reflections*, Mem Fox summarizes the importance of a writing group to a teacher of writing.

> *How do I, as a teacher, organize myself to write? I have a group of six friends, all of whom teach writing, who provide me with an audience at least one evening a month, over nibbles and coffee, or stronger. We share our pieces about home, work, life, children, colleagues, hopes, memories, and so on in an atmosphere of noncompetitive trust. If it weren't for the writing group, I would hardly write at all, because I need an audience so badly. The purpose is to entertain, persuade, inform, and just share. My deadline is usually met a couple of hours before we are due to meet—most of us write only in the twenty-four hours before our meeting. If we need the*

group to confer with us on an important article or submission, the group is happy to do it. We laugh over our wickedness in presenting first drafts most of the time. We grin over the fact that some pieces are unfinished because they were only begun a few hours previously. We give critical help seriously when it is asked for. What we all know is that we would never write, outside the requirements of our work, if we didn't have the group to write for. (1993, 40-41)

With the professional and personal demands of my life, I know that I will not write for myself without the deadline of a writing group to get me started and the fellowship of a writing group to keep me going. There is the very real danger of slipping into the familiar and, I admit, more comfortable mode of not writing.

Remarkably, I found myself beginning to think like a writer—a goal that Donald Graves stresses for students in writing workshop and a state I never really understood completely until I experienced it. I found myself thinking in terms of topics I'd like to write about and doing "what if" exercises in my head. The day I was mulling over a problem in my head and heard myself say, "I am not sure what I really think about this, so I'd better write about it," I knew I had truly achieved a writer's perspective.

Viewing myself as a writer was a key transition in my thinking. Now, if someone asks me whether I'm a writer, I reply in the affirmative and bite my tongue before I am tempted to add the irrelevant information that I'm a beginning writer in many genres and am far from skilled.

During this past year I have discovered more reasons to write than I would have thought possible, and I have become addicted. Donald Murray explains this condition: "This is the writer's addiction: we write because we surprise ourselves, educate ourselves, entertain ourselves. Writing, we see more, feel more, think more, understand more than when we are not writing in our head or on the page" (1985, 7).

One of my colleagues has drawn up a list of at least thirty purposes writing can serve, including to persuade, to inform, to entertain, and to question, but unless we experience and pass on to our students our enthusiasm for writing, they will continue to avoid writing for any purpose. Murray offers the following advice to writing teachers:

[A]lways behind each writing purpose is the secret excitement of discovery: the word, the line, the sentence, the page that achieves its own life and its own meaning. The first

responsibility of the writing teacher is to experience this essential surprise. You can't teach what you don't know. (1995, 8)

Before, I wouldn't have understood what Murray is saying, but now my personal goal in my English classroom is to provide as many opportunities as possible for my students to experience that surprise, which is both self-affirming and irresistible.

My Classroom

My experiences as a writer led to profound changes in my classroom. I now view myself as a facilitator rather than as a pontificator, meaning that I no longer have to pretend to have all the answers. By writing with my students, I convey my view that all of us are writers, and I can anticipate the difficulties the students may have with a particular assignment. When I share problems that I'm having, I demonstrate that writing is not easy and that it is always evolving. When I honestly ask for their input, I demonstrate my respect for their opinions and model one way in which writers may try to solve problems in their writing.

I have a short story in process that I can't seem to finish, perhaps because the content is too close to a painful experience in my life. I presented that story to my sophomore English classes, saying only that I was having a problem with it. After reading the story aloud and explaining what I was trying to convey to the reader, I asked for suggestions. There was a what-are-we-supposed-to-say kind of silence and then a few vague comments such as "It's good" or "It's fine."

Searching for a way to elicit the type of response I'd hoped for, I told the class that my specific problem was coming up with a satisfactory ending. Then hands went up, and suggestions, some good and some awful, came flying at me. After listening carefully to all of their comments, I thanked the students and said I would consider some of their ideas and share any results with them. Clearly, my students were flattered by my request for help and responded eagerly when I made it more specific.

I try to enhance the feeling of cooperation and promote the attitude that we are all learning, experimenting, and growing through writing groups, peer conferences, and teacher conferences. When students approach me with a problem, I ask questions rather than give definite answers: *What feeling do you want to create here? What are some ways you might achieve that? Did you know that Sally had a similar problem with her poem last week? Why don't you ask her what she tried?* Though I offer suggestions, I make it clear that most of the time there are no instant solutions and that the teacher doesn't have all the answers. At times the temptation to revert to the authority role is strong, but I always insist that the student writers, though they may consult with others and solicit their opinions, must make the final decisions.

Of course, the teacher still carries the mantle of expertise in the students' minds, but in the writing classroom I use that expertise to validate student writing. As Ralph Fletcher points out, the writing teacher patiently endures all the unsuccessful efforts and "picks out moments when the writing works well" (1993, 14). I find myself constantly seeking the word, the phrase, the comparison, the description that will place the writer in the literary limelight. Fletcher adds, "Even in bad pieces of writing, the mentor reaches into the chaos, finds a place where the writing works, pulls it from the wreckage, names it, and makes the writer aware of this emerging skill with words. Careful praise of this kind can fuel a writer for a long time" (14). In this instance I am again modeling the type of response I expect students to give each other.

Young writers soon realize that expressing their ideas and creating a framework for those ideas is a difficult and often frustrating business. Sometimes nothing works. Ryan came to me with a problem line in a poem she had just written. "It's just not right, and I don't know why," she said, pointing to the line in question. If I were still playing my role of teacher as final authority, I would have said, "Well, it's obvious that the rhythm is way off. You need to change some words." Now I no longer assume or prescribe. Instead, I asked her to read the poem aloud to see if she would recognize how and where the rhythm broke down. She didn't. "Maybe it needs a different word arrangement," I suggested. She experimented and did improve the rhythm, but in the end rejected all the new lines. She conferred with a classmate and still didn't arrive at a change she felt was "right." In the end she left the line as it was, saying even as she proofread the typed copy before it became part of the class literary booklet, "It's still not right." Based on my own struggles with poetry, I could assure her that she would eventually find the words she was seeking and could change her poem at that time. By allowing Ryan the freedom to seek suggestions as well as the freedom to reject those same suggestions, I ensured that she saw the poem and any decisions concerning it as hers.

Though in the majority of cases the responsibility for revisions remains with the student, there are times when I ask a student to revise for a definite purpose, and when I assume my role of final editor, I insist on the conventions of written English. A student who wants to forego these conventions must present sound reasons.

Getting Started

At the beginning of the school year, very few of my students wrote for pleasure, and most viewed writing as an unpleasant experience foisted upon them by demented English teachers. Many professed to hate writing and told me forcefully that they couldn't write (translation: I feel I am not good at this). I could certainly sympathize with their feelings of inadequacy as well as with their view that writing is an unpleasant experience, because I had been there myself all too recently. Just as I had needed encouragement, tasks at which I could succeed, and a supportive audience to find the unique sparks in my writing, so my students needed the opportunity to experiment and succeed with their writing in a positive environment.

To that end I began with brief writings and formula poems such as headline poems and found poems, pieces that established us as writers who are always seeking the startling and effective phrase or word combination. As I had observed in my own writing groups, some students took off running while others were more hesitant and needed to be encouraged, coaxed, praised, prodded, and pushed to get beyond the warm-up.

Group Work

When we had established writing as part of our routine, I introduced the concept of the writing groups where students could listen, find the parts of the piece that really worked, and offer suggestions. Some groups were more successful than others, but I felt we were making real progress when some of the students began to complain that their writing groups weren't helping them. B.J. was typical: "My group is useless. They just say my story is fine as it is."

From my experiences as part of a writing group, I understood what B.J. was saying. As my confidence in my writing increased and I could better judge which parts of a piece worked and which didn't, I looked to my group for more than just praise. In fact, I began to distrust commentary that was only positive. "Tell me what isn't working and what I need to work on," I wanted to say. Like B.J., I recognized that saying a piece is "fine" is the easy way out, but it does not fulfill the larger responsibility each member has to the group. When a member of my own writing group says that she doesn't understand a passage or questions an image or a word choice, she demonstrates that she has taken the time to read and reflect upon what I have written. Because of my experiences I understood the nature of the problem and presented a minilesson that demonstrated effective group and peer responses.

Grammar

Instead of looking at grammar and usage as compulsory units to be taught because next year's teacher would expect it, I found myself looking at grammar and usage as tools a writer uses to enhance effective communication. Initially my students were taken aback by my questions: "Do you want the reader to pause at the end of this line or keep going?" "How long do you want the pause to be?" "What mark of punctuation tells the reader that an explanation follows?" "Can you see why this is called a dangling modifier and may confuse the reader?" As soon as they realized that their choices were significant, they accepted the responsibility readily. We practiced punctuation skills in our poetry drafts and reviewed the conventions for dialogue by writing, with a partner, an entire plot in dialogue.

Literature

My experiences as a writer also changed my approach to teaching literature. Instead of plowing through an anthology, "translating" the stories, poems, and plays, we read trade books that held the students' interest. We looked for those elements of the writing that worked well. After analyzing why a writer succeeded and what techniques he or she used, we practiced those techniques ourselves. When we studied fiction, the students created an imaginary character and then described that character, in a first-person character sketch and through the eyes of the character's acquaintances (both friend and foe) and possessions. The next assignment asked the writer to present the character to the reader solely through a description of his possession. Finally, the students created plots that could grow logically from the character's life.

In our classroom, literature and writing complemented each other. We wrote in imitation of blues poems and interior monologues and for our found poems searched for powerful words and phrases in Elie Wiesel's *Night* and John Steinbeck's *The Pearl.* We found passages in our independently chosen books that impressed or moved us and shared these with the class. Throughout, we focused on writing that connects strongly with the reader through precise imagery and clarity of expression.

Publishing

My writing experiences also convinced me of the importance of "publishing," or going public with our writing. In April we picked our best poems, hung them on small "poet trees," which the classes decorated, and sent them out to other classrooms, inviting them to add their own poetry. The trees and the poems were an unqualified success: they were displayed in the Media Center and even featured in a local paper. We displayed our favorite pieces on a special wall in the Media Center designated as "The Writer's Corner." I also created a notebook for each class using a large three-ring binder. Each student created a title page for his or her section and kept published work there during the year. The notebooks were available to all the students as idea banks or for reading.

As the school year ended, I reviewed my successes and failures. I still had students who said English was boring and dumb, but I had more who were actively involved with language in a positive way, and this would not have occurred if I had remained an observer of writing, rather than becoming a participant. Seventeen years of teaching tell me that what I am now doing is the best method for teaching writing, and that if I want to be a credible writing teacher, I must write.

"What Do I Do on Monday (and Tuesday, Wednesday, Thursday, and Friday)?": Experimenting with Workshop Teaching

Whole Language and Process Teaching Meet the Secondary Classroom

Teachers of English and language arts in grades 7–12 must deal with a set of pressures beyond those outlined in the introduction to Part 1. These pressures grow out of the changes that elementary and college-level writing and reading instruction have undergone over the past decade or more, and they pose a different, and in some ways thornier, set of problems for middle and high school teachers. Specifically, whole language has grown in popularity in the primary and upper elementary grades at the same time that college and university first-year writing courses have embraced writing as a process and critical reading as their pedagogical focuses. Whole language and process teaching share many basic tenets:

- People learn best when they are engaged in meaningful activities in meaningful contexts (i.e., they learn to write by writing to real audiences and to read by reading stories, poems, essays, and books, rather than by doing skills exercises or reading disconnected excerpts).

- Writers of any age engage in activities, such as invention, drafting, revising, conferring, and editing, that can be taught and practiced, rather than engaging in the traditional practice of assigned writing and graded final drafts.

- Writing can be a way of generating ideas, not just recording them; reading is an active process of constructing meaning, not merely decoding words.

- Students perform best when they have freedom to choose what to write and read, instead of having to complete assignments that hold no interest for them.

- Students can learn a great deal from one another—as sounding boards, sympathetic but critical readers, and collaborators—instead of working quietly at their desks alone.

- The teacher's role is to create structured situations in which students work, independently or together, to learn, not to be the center of attention in the classroom while students listen passively.

These tenets lead to the sort of classroom characterized by workshop teaching. They have their roots in observations of people's behavior outside school—how young children learn to speak, and what experienced or professional writers do when they compose. This interest in students' behavior while learning reflects a commonality of purpose among primary teachers and first-year writing teachers: both are helping neophytes learn how to survive in a new educational environment.

For secondary teachers, however, this has not traditionally been the case. Middle school teachers must also initiate students into a new system, but they inherit a trend that starts in fourth grade and is full-blown by ninth or tenth grade: an increasing emphasis on subject matter. Secondary teachers tend to look not to elementary teachers or to teachers of first-year college courses as kindred spirits, but to identify with their college professors, the ones who teach Shakespeare, Milton, Whitman, and Emerson. And why not? In English, as in most subjects, 7–12 certification programs closely mirror traditional English (that is to say, *literature*) majors in their requirements, and most middle schools and high schools are structured according to subject, just as colleges are. Their curriculums reinforce this identification, often stipulating a broad range of content that students in each secondary grade must master (or at least read and take a test on) in order to pass. I've heard it said on more than one occasion that elementary teachers teach students, while college teachers teach subjects. Once again, secondary teachers are somewhere in between.

Whole Teaching

Since most teachers care deeply about their students *and* their subjects, their position is often uncomfortable. This discomfort is heightened by the competing claims of educational programs and philosophies, which seldom recognize teachers' need to adapt instruction to their students and to themselves. As Kathy McDonell, a Change Course! participant, explains:

> *For the last few years, I had truly created my own philosophy of education, one balancing my experiences in my own classroom as a teacher and student and those experiences as a student in others' classrooms. This philosophy, I found, was more of a patchwork quilt of approaches and beliefs than a unifed comforter. Given this, I had grown weary of reading about and hearing about THE WAYs: whole language, assertive discipline, process writing, back-to-basics, portfolio assessment, phonics, etc. . . . Why? Because many times those who were not complete disciples of the particular approach were made out to be lesser teachers, unenlightened teachers, even poor teachers. It appeared to me that teachers were expected to tailor their methodologies to students' individual needs and learning styles, and at the same time, if a particular approach didn't suit a particular teacher, too bad. In essence, our students' unique personalities were to be respected; ours as teachers weren't.* (1995, 3–4)

McDonell learned that much teacher distress stems from society's expectation that teachers "create learning environments conducive to students' needs only." In contrast she quotes Greta Nagel in *The Tao of Teaching:* "Wise teachers choose their courses to fit their personalities. What may be too intense for one person can be a normal opportunity for another. The teacher who suffers from burnout is often one who did not know to choose personal priorities well" (Nagel 147, quoted in McDonell 5).

Successful teachers, then, learn what they do well and build on those elements. They pick and choose from among various methods, materials, and philosophies to develop curriculums that balance their students' needs and their own. If "whole language" is based on respect for learners, what successful teachers do might be called "whole teaching," because it also respects their needs.

The chapters in this section embody "whole teaching" at its best. The authors speak with the authority of years of successful teaching, and the essays begin from positions of strength and confidence. These people knew they were good teachers, yet they felt that they could be better by adapting workshop methods to their classrooms—and "adapting" is the operative word here. As Paula Lochotzki explains, her method was to look for places where she could "exchange" one practice for another, so that she could maintain her overall sense of her classroom and its goals but sub-stitute more appropriate practices for less useful ones. Debra Ciambro Grisso and Richard D. Hughes, on the other hand, focus on the process: what does a teacher who is trying to initiate changes do to make those changes come about? I read Grisso's essay as a lesson in patience, in giving an innovation enough time and thought to make it effective. Hughes's piece shows clearly that no educational practice will be a universal pana-cea, but that a practice is well worth keeping if it helps more students learn than what it replaces. Innovative teaching is often held to a higher standard than traditional practices, and this essay refutes the common no-tion that an innovation must work for every student.

Finally, Cheryl H. Almeda traces the development of a writing work-shop within a flexible sophomore English class and a fairly traditional, se-nior British literature course, showing how peer sharing can be made to work with, not against, curricular demands for "content." She demon-strates the falsity of the misconception that a teacher must adopt a philos-ophy or method whole.

These four chapters also demonstrate the fruitfulness of critically exam-ining curriculums and teaching practices. At all levels of education teach-ers are asked to teach their students to do "critical thinking," which John Dewey defined as posing problems and solving them (Bean 1996, 2). In these chapters, the teachers identify problems in their teaching: lack of student engagement, inadequate responses to reading, chaotic peer con-ferences, poor audience awareness and motivation to write well; and set about solving those problems using workshop techniques. Although self-examination of this sort seems threatening, their voices resonate with the pleasure and pride that engaged critical thought can and should en-gender. In their classrooms, then, they model for their students "the natu-ral, healthy, and motivating pleasure of problems" (Bean 1996, 2), adding value to their already valuable teaching.

Nuts and Bolts

The essays in this section do more than show how changing from traditional to workshop teaching can take place. They also present a wealth of ideas and practices that teachers wishing to "do workshop" can adapt to their own situations. Paula Lochotzki's chapter, "The Great Exchange," offers a comprehensive overview of workshop teaching. Pinpointing the practices she needs to revise to become a more effective teacher, Paula describes how she devises themes for her course, how she orchestrates writing workshop and learns to trust reading workshop, how she charts students' growth through the year, and how she fosters self-assessment and the compiling of portfolios. Throughout, she offers samples of student writing that illustrate some of the responses such practices make possible and act as models of good response.

The three chapters that follow are more focused on particular practices. Debra Ciambro Grisso's essay concerns the best ways to foster thoughtful student responses to literature. Through examples of both good and poor responses, Debbie shows the advantages and drawbacks of various journal writing assignments and, ultimately, how to make letter-writing between students and teacher possible. She also demonstrates some ways in which minilessons can be used to create sequences of assignments and to experiment with teaching.

"Falling Off the Skateboard," Richard D. Hughes's chapter, explores peer conferences in a typical eighth-grade classroom. Ric describes necessary preconditions for success in such a classroom, where students are, as my ninth grade English teacher used to say, "just on the verge of becoming human." He discusses how to form—and re-form—groups to make them functional, describes the types of groups that may emerge and their dynamics, and shares his experience with a student who proved unable to work in any group.

Cheryl H. Almeda offers advice on moving beyond peer conferences in high school classrooms to forms of sharing in which the whole class is an audience for students' writing. She discusses reading aloud as a way to motivate students, reward them, and celebrate their writing; setting up poetry competitions within a classroom to determine "Best of Row"; and oral presentations in which students share poems by published poets with one another. As do all these chapters, hers includes samples of student work and students' reactions to these activities.

Together, these essays show teachers exploring their teaching and looking for ways to make a good thing better. They show how they balance their students' needs, curricular requirements, and their own needs within their particular teaching contexts as they play with elements of workshop teaching. These teachers demonstrate the truth that McDonell identifies: teaching students demands teaching ourselves (1995, 5), and changing course in our classrooms demands that we learn as our students learn.

CHAPTER 4

The Great Exchange

Paula Lochotzki

Are you aware of gaps in your teaching? Do you have spaces in your sense of your discipline that professional reading, swapping ideas with other teachers, or taking courses cannot fill? If so, you and I have something in common. This something was revealed to me in part in my students' evaluations. I teach five classes—a hundred and twenty sophomore girls, with their mercurial mood swings, self-centeredness, and earthiness, their longings and regrets, their birthday countdowns and anniversaries of friendships or breakups. These are the students who live for the weekend, the phone, their driver's license, for friends and friendship, and it is somewhere in and between this melancholy and this idealism that they seek identity and freedom. In recent years I have been getting the same responses on their evaluations: "Yes, we write a great deal—but you never let us write about what is important to us." And "You never give us time to read." I tried, in vain, to rationalize my methods, but in my heart, I was as disgruntled as they were. In assessing my methods, I pinpointed four that led to results I didn't want:

1. *My students didn't write what was important to them.* Yes, my students wrote a great deal, usually in response to a work of literature according to a prompt or a choice of prompts that *I* generated. They did a minimum of peer editing and then produced a final draft, which I meticulously corrected.

2. *I took charge of their writing.* Often I spent more time editing a single paper than the student did in writing it. My comments were prescriptive: "If you do A, B, and C, then you will have a fine paper." But the paper was no longer theirs: it was mine.

Often they complained about and criticized my comments. (How could

39

they misconstrue my good intentions?) The results, however, never varied. Once I returned the papers, their mood changed: sullen silences. Angry disbelief. Some stuffed their papers inside their notebooks, never to look at them again; others simply threw them away.

3. *I didn't allow enough time for reading.* I had tried requiring book reports on suggested book titles. Many would read the required books, but other students worked equally hard to write the report without reading at all. I wanted them to enjoy reading, to make connections, to love words, but if this was occurring, it was not obvious to me.

4. *I didn't fully utilize portfolio assessment.* I wanted to know how each student was growing as a writer and a reader. Unfortunately, I didn't even know how to grade "Amy" as Amy; I only knew how to grade Amy in relation to twenty-five other students! How could I individualize my evaluations? An idea that was good in theory involved too much paper-shuffling and bookkeeping.

Because I had taken a brief workshop on portfolio assessment and read a few essays in books and periodicals, I thought I knew all about assessment. I saved students' papers for them and then, every quarter or semester, asked them to review their work and answer a few questions. The students dutifully looked through their papers (the ones they had not disposed of in fits of anger), responded tersely to my questions, and selected two pieces to place in their folders to send on to the next class. I was disappointed that they didn't display more pride in their work. After all, I had put so much time into their papers!

My Premises: To Awaken Sleeping Writers and Thinkers

- Within each of us there is a writer. It is my privilege to awaken that sleeping writer and lead her to experience the power of words.

- We are all gifted; only the context determines the evidence.

- Such learning, a process of discovery and of making connections, should be exciting. My goal is to instill a lifelong love of learning and to enhance a feeling of self-worth.

- Every encounter and experience contains a seed of learning.

- Not so much what we learn, but our insights about ourselves make the difference.

- How we teach, not what we teach, builds thinking skills.

Students will grow more as thinkers through everyday interactions than through a special class or curriculum on critical thinking. I have a mirror in my classroom; beneath it is a sign that reads, "Behold the one responsible for your education." Who is teacher? Who is learner?

I knew these things in theory but my students did not always experience them in my classroom. I was so bogged down by content, by curriculum, by piling up of bits of information, that I seldom got around to demonstrating how to think about what we were learning.

Exchanges

I like to view my new way of teaching not as so many changes but as a set of exchanges. I exchanged my fifty-minute lectures for minilessons of five to ten minutes. I exchanged "harangues" on grammar and the technicalities of writing for individual conferences with students. Before, I knew that reading aloud to students was important, but I was always in search of just the right book and just the right time, and neither presented itself very often. I exchanged not reading for *daily* reading. I exchanged a genre-based course plan of isolated units on short story, drama, poetry, and essays for one based on thematic units. I exchanged my teacher-proposed writing topics for individual, student-selected topics and my reading lists for student-selected books. Finally, I exchanged my assessments for theirs. These exchanges have made a difference by filling the gap between my methods and my desired goals.

Tracing Three Students

As the weeks of the first year of my new, "exchanged" curriculum unfolded, I observed three students, recording jottings in my personal journal, making notes on student-teacher and student-student conferences, my observations, our interviews, and my evaluations, and examining their portfolios.

Because of the diverse student culture in our school, I chose Alisha, who was from India. She was introverted and her writing showed she already had a sensitivity for words.

I chose Laney because she was a dreamer. She walked and talked slowly, and was generally pensive. When I asked her the question "What is a writer?" she answered with a drawing, a succession of flowing, curving lines. I was struck by her total concentration. When she showed me her picture, she said simply, "Real writers put their soul into their writing, and this represents the soul of a writer."

Finally, I chose Kathy because she was fun-loving, friendly, athletic, inquisitive, and, like all teenagers, sensitive. She seemed representative of many of my students. These three students helped me understand what was happening in my changed classroom.

From Genres to Themes

Exchanging genre-based teaching units for thematic units was a significant change. The traditional genre approach "worked," and it allowed me to present a great deal of literature to the students along with writing. But they didn't always see the connections between the selections or between the selections and their own lives. Instead of teaching short stories first quarter, poetry second, drama third, and novels fourth, I selected meaningful material around important themes: *driving, freedom, choices,* and *conflict.* I added *making connections.* Now we focus on a different theme each quarter: "Making Connections Between Literature and My Life"; "Driving Forces—What Motivates People"; "Making Choices in Life"; and "Resolving Conflict" and consider related poetry, drama, short stories, and novels.

A Blueprint for Change

Next I drew up "A Do-It-Yourself Integrated Language Arts Planning Guide" (Figure 1; adapted from Eisele 1991, 64). This guide stretched my thinking about my curriculum as no other device or incentive had. In an oval in the middle was the single word *Theme.* I penciled in my first theme: "Making Connections Between Literature and My Life." Around the oval, connecting lines led to a number of boxes with the titles *Student Reading, Teacher Read-Alouds, Nonfiction Selections, Writing Skills for Minilessons, Speaking and Drama Activities, Writing Activities, Projects, Music, Art, Media, Fun Activities to Introduce Theme,* and *Assessment.*

As I filled in the boxes, working with my own resources and tapping the expertise of other teachers, I realized that I did not need to teach every short story, every poem, and every essay in the book. Thus, making connections for the students was simplified because I was making connections. Then, since I was not teaching as many individual pieces of literature, I was free to introduce new things, namely, reading and writing workshop. Mondays and Tuesdays became writing workshop days,

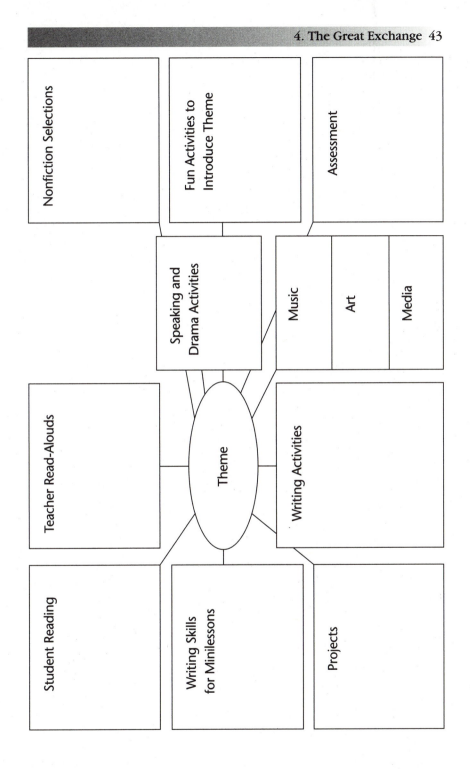

Theme

Nonfiction Selections

Fun Activities to Introduce Theme

Assessment

Speaking and Drama Activities

Music

Art

Media

Teacher Read-Alouds

Writing Activities

Student Reading

Writing Skills for Minilessons

Projects

Wednesdays and Thursdays literature days, and Fridays reading workshop days.

Writing Workshop

On Mondays and Tuesdays, I read a children's book, a poem, a personal piece of writing, a passage from a book, or an article from a newspaper to my students. Then I presented a five- to ten-minute minilesson on some aspect of writing—such as how to confer, using dialogue, showing not telling, beginnings, transitions, or endings. Next, we briefly discussed, in pairs or small groups, how they could draw on their own experiences, and then they used the remainder of the period for writing. Knowing that by Thursday they needed to turn in a five-page double-spaced draft kept the students focused. Although they wrote brief responses to what I had read as a way to tap into their experiences, ultimately they chose their own topics.

Even after our general survey of genres, many students were hesitant about writing without some kind of prompt, despite my encouragement. Kathy wrote,

> *When I found out we weren't going to be given any prompts, I was puzzled as to what to write. I wondered if you were trying reverse psychology on us. Naturally I was expecting to have to write about my summer vacation—how boring. But this time it was different. I couldn't stop thinking about my summer vacation. Soon I produced one of my most effective pieces, "On Top of the World." It came from my experience and it was genuine.*

Because I was strong on expository and persuasive writing, giving students direction but no specific prompts was a stretch for all of us. Would it work? Would they write? I found support in Tom Romano's *Writing with Passion,* in which he observes that expository writing too narrowly defines the nature of acceptable academic writing: "Good writing, regardless of the mode of discourse, causes writers to think. That thinking involves a productive dialectic between analysis and synthesis" (1995, 6).

I encouraged the students to explore their inner and outer worlds in a way that they had never done before and at a time in their lives when searching for identity was their main task.

Because I was curious about how they were coming up with topics, I asked Laney how she picked hers. She wrote,

> *"Desert" was born pretty much the way in which all my stories are born. I see a picture in my mind's eye and within milliseconds, I see a story. Obviously I am anxious to write this all down before my mind turns to crumbling ashes and the words elude me (as words like to do), leaving me breathless, confused, and grasping at the air for some shred of comprehension of the saga that momentarily consumed me. So I take out my pen (it has to be MY PEN) and write, and write. Before long, "Desert" is born—draft one. Next I alternate between peer and self-conferencing, teacher and self-conferencing. Dilemma: to be true to myself or to be true to my audience? Every time I write, I give a piece of myself away. Eventually I suppose, I'll become empty and shriveled but then I will simply gather up my many stories and chew on them and consume them as they consumed me.*

Laney wrote this response during the first quarter. That she and the other students were writing about what was important to them became a given. They explored their loves, hates, disappointments, memories, dreams, friends, and friendship.

Laney wrote a poem in response to Picasso's painting of a man holding a guitar:

The Old Guitarist

> *He sits,*
> *listens to the ocean,*
> *echoing the lost distant thoughts of his memories.*
> *He closes his eyes,*
> *and remembers;*
> *the person he might have been,*
> *the person he never was,*
> *the lovers he might have kept,*
> *the daughter who might have kept him.*
> *It is too late to regret.*
>
> *As the cold, surging rush of water*
> *caresses his mind and his ears,*

he wonders what it would be like to throw his body,
his self,
into those waters,
to fly,
if only for a moment
to live
if only for a moment without regard, and without the weight
of his past.

What's done is done.

In the depth of the icy, liquid abyss
would he find himself, waiting below the surface
to drag him
with the gnarled, arthritic hands of a guitarist, like a mighty
twisted ancient oak,
down to the bottom where he would drown in the sorrows of
the sky?

His fingers,
cracked, knotted, callused
skillfully stroke, and pick the strings of the old guitar.
Each note piercing the air
then lingering, hanging, and slowly trailing like an effulgent
fire cracker,
the volume penetrating his ears.

And as he sits there,
thinking no great thoughts that were never thought before,
playing the music of an old man
an old guitarist;
He makes the waves sing.

As writers do, though she wrote of a guitarist, she revealed a bit of herself.

For the last seven or eight minutes of class, I invited students to the front of the classroom to share a few lines of what they had written. These brief exchanges led to improved writing. Often the oooh's, the quick intake of breath, or the laughter was sufficient feedback to keep the writers writing. And I accepted whatever they read or honored their wish to pass. Soon they began to applaud each other's efforts, to offer words of encouragement. Through peer conferences they summarized each other's papers; they learned the art of asking questions; they looked for logic and unity; and they offered alternatives. By the end of the first quarter many students were beginning to identify themselves as writers.

Reading Workshop

Reading workshop was a great way to wind down the week. Kathy spoke for many students when she said, "I like the relaxed atmosphere of English class, especially on Fridays when we can just come in and read whatever we want and not have to worry about the stress of a test. What a way to end the week!"

On Fridays students turned in one to three pages of their reading logs in which they responded to books they had chosen to read during their two hours of outside reading each week. Sometimes I looked at their logs and other times they exchanged and read each others. Kathy admitted,

> *At first, I did not like the idea of all this reading. Now that my writing has improved, however, I wondered how it happened. Besides the great amount of writing we did, I realized that by reading so much, it did affect my writing. I usually don't show my feelings, but while responding to my reading I let my feelings flow. I felt safe knowing that I won't be docked if I didn't agree with the author. Sometimes I even wrote about how angry I was and that was all right, too. I love the freedom of reading whatever I want to. Before I only read when I absolutely had to read but now I read because I want to and often on Fridays I am the first to sit on a pillow, ready and eager to read.*

I will admit that I was initially dubious about reading workshop, wondering if students would really use their time to read. My concern was short-lived. The quiet was one indicator. I circulated among the students and noted their reading selections, thinking that some would try to use the time for a study hall, but this happened only rarely. Thus I, too, settled into reading. The students liked this quiet time and were free to sit anywhere in the room. On average, each student read about four books per quarter.

Progress: An Index Card

Another part of my writing program called for charting each student's growth on an index card. Formerly, when I made corrections on student papers, I summarized the major types of errors or weaknesses and addressed each class accordingly. At that point, however, I was not at all certain who didn't understand paragraphing, or thesis statements, or transitions, or the correct spelling of *too,* although it didn't really matter. I delivered my "harangue" and hoped that the "grammar culprit" knew I was speaking to her. I felt better after such deliveries, but never once in twenty-five years did the fragments become less fragmented, or did the commas and quotations fall into place.

So, an index card could do what multiple corrections and lectures didn't do? Yes. After I returned a set of papers on Mondays, I conferred briefly with each student (I could get through a class of twenty-six students in two days). With only positive comments and a grade, how differently the students received their papers! While the others were writing or conferring, I called each student to sit next to me. She held her paper and an index card. Again I reiterated what I liked about the paper and then chose one or two points that would move her writing forward.

Initially, Kathy's problem was organization. We talked about it one-on-one in conjunction with her paper. She listened, and on her index card she wrote the date and the word "organization." I asked her if she could define "organization."

She wrote, "Think new."

"Think new"? I asked.

"Yes. When I write, I know the story. I have to think like I didn't. I have to think new and write my information so it makes sense to my readers."

I asked her if she would be willing to work on organization in her next paper. She agreed. When she turned in her next paper, she placed this index card on top, and as I read it, I graded especially for organization. I drew a smiley face and wrote a brief comment and dated it. The card became a continuous record of her individual progress, one I shared during parent-teacher conferences.

Quest for Identity

Sophomores relentlessly pursue the self-absorbed task of searching for an identity. It is a time to remember and a time to dream, to risk and to be secure, to be passionate and bored. Unlike our fast-paced society, which does not encourage self-reflection, the reading and writing workshops gave students invaluable opportunities to explore their inner thoughts and feelings and their outer world. I was amazed at the amount of writing they had done: five pages of writing drafts plus between one and three pages of reading logs weekly for four quarters was quite impressive. I was surprised at the breadth and depth of topics they chose, the connections they made, the insights they had, and the questions they asked.

Writer's Response

Kathy liked to write fiction. When she began a story, she often made four to six drafts. (Before, I could scarcely get students to do even a second draft.) In her first-quarter assessment she wrote, "My pieces range from death oto peanut butter and jelly sandwiches." Her style was simple and straightforward. In an earlier evaluation of her writing, Kathy wrote,

> *I have experienced real writing this year. What a contrast to other years in which I wandered in Dood-Da Land writing about things that weren't relevant, writing about things the teacher thought were important, writing about things that would bore the stripes right off a zebra!"*

Alisha preferred poetry. This was the first year she had ever written "real poetry"—poetry that was not modeled or formulated. She noted,

> *I'm not sure at what point it happened, but I became aware, really aware of the writer within me. You said in the beginning of the year that you believed we all had one, but I didn't believe you. But she's really there and she has things to share. Time has definitely helped me. Never before was I given a longer time to just sit and write, so I was never able to explore my talent. At last I am in touch with a very special part of me.*

I was struck by the questions students pursued. Although she referred to herself as "the ponderer," Kathy's questions, as in this log entry, were often superficial:

> *Why can't our world be carefree as a beautiful, majestic dolphin? How many people really wear seatbelts? Why would anyone not wear one? Why don't drivers put their blinker on when they want to turn? Why don't they turn the blinker off? . . . When you die, you go to heaven FOREVER. That's a very long time. I can't get over the fact that I'll be there forever!*

There is no end to forever. Why is the sky blue, not orange or the grass not purple? How did they come up with the alphabet and numbers? Finally, can people breathe and talk at the same time?

In contrast, Alisha's questions were critical. In a poem, "Hypocrite in the Mirror," she addresses her father:

You dictate your orders like Allah himself
to everyone around you as if they are holy truths.
"Do this . . .
"Do that . . .
But tell me this:
Do you follow what you say?
Are not your decrees applicable to you also?

You tell me to be kind to my siblings and others.
"Don't fight!"
"Be compassionate."
But wasn't it last night when you
verbally attacked my own mother?
You readily preach to me the word of the Holy Book
its message of love and patience.
But was it not just this morning when out of anger and
    frustration
you threatened to hit my own brother?

You tell me to listen to what you have to say.
"Show respect."
But when I try to voice my side of the story,
do you listen?
You don't even care to hear it.

You tell me to look in the mirror
and see what kind of person I really am.
But sometime . . . just once
I think you should turn the mirror around
and take a look at you.

Do you mean what you say?
If so, why do you do what you do?

Are your intentions heartfelt
Or are they intended for display?

When you will change,
or if you ever will
I do not know.
Maybe it will take days, weeks, months, or years
for you to reflect upon the face in your mirror.

In her reading, Alisha wondered what certain characters were feeling and often identified with them. Reflecting on N. H. Kleinbaum's novel, *Dead Poets Society,* she noted, "I'm beginning to notice that Todd is very withdrawn. I wonder what he's feeling. I'm becoming attached to Neil's character. He's so nice to include Todd and push him to be involved when no one else seems to care. I could use somebody like that in my life. . . .'"

Change Your Diet

Laney was mesmerized by the horror stories of R. L. Stine. She read horror, wrote it, and even dreamed about it. After Laney spent a semester reading and writing horrific stories, I suggested that she challenge herself and choose a completely different genre, knowing that she could still return to Rice, Stine, and Plath. To my delight and amazement she picked up Alan Lightman's *Einstein's Dreams.* In her log, she wrote that she was enthralled with Einstein and considered him to be her "soul mate," boasting that many of his theories were already hers. She pondered extremes.

> *I am fascinated by the numbers 0 and infinity. The total absence, and the total presence. The void and the richness. The dark and the light. Black and white. Never and forever. The beginning and . . . the end? The eternal continuation of the beginning. The virgin time and all the possibilities.*

She theorized:

> *My theory is that the universe is infinite. I can explain this by reminding one that by "the universe," I mean the expanse of existence. Not just the stars and planets. Is there a point somewhere where things cease to exist? If so, what is beyond that point? Nothing? Even nothing is something, isn't it? It ex-*

ists, doesn't it? If nothing did not exist, then it would be something, wouldn't it? So, whether nothing is nothing or something, it exists and I am correct. Now the universe is infinite because even if there stops being something and there is nothing then the nothing would go on forever. . . .

I don't know. You're the one who asked me what I was thinking yesterday.

Making Meaning, Exploring Identity

I wanted students to find meaning in their lives. In the writing and reading workshops, they enjoyed time to pursue the timeless questions of identity. In fact, they created a long paper trail of thoughts, feelings, and reactions. In a student assessment at the end of third quarter, I asked them to reread their writing drafts and reading logs and identify the question underlying all of their writing. Then they were to write themselves a letter identifying the question and answer it.

Alisha wrote,

> *What am I feeling?*
> *What is the fountainhead in which I dip my emotional ink?*
> *Each word scrawled has an emotion attached*
> *like a puppet's strings.*
> *Anger spurs bitter words;*
> *Happiness pours joyful script;*
> *Sorrow casts words shadowed with tears.*
> *Feelings seen in print*
> *unleash similar feelings.*

I responded, "Alisha, you have the heart of a poet! I wish I had penned these lines! Write on!"

Playing with paradox, Laney wrote herself this letter:

> *You question me (though it's more making a point of than asking) about the difference between the light and the dark. You question me about the difference between goodness and evil. You ask at what point does love mingle hate, pain hint at satisfaction, pure love become dark love, the boundary between life and death. The only answer I can give you is shadow.*

Asking these questions is like asking for the meaning of life. If you look deep enough, you will see that there is no black and white, there are no boundaries anywhere; these things are intertwined and tangled, wrestling and suffocating each other, and in-between is a hazy oblivion.

The love of Satan, the pleasure of pain, the beauty of homicidal ugliness, the sorrow of the perfect glory. This is the way that the world truly exists. Welcome to oblivion. You have found your way home.

Look What I Have Done!

Who better to assess her own personal growth than the student herself? Going through a student's portfolio is a thrilling experience. It is one thing for me to recognize growth by giving a higher number grade, another for the student to see and verbalize how her writing has changed and developed.

Each quarter I asked the students to reread their drafts and their reading logs and to assess their own progress as readers and writers. Next, I asked them to place all of their drafts in order from the most to the least effective and posed some basic questions: What made your best piece so effective? What could you still do to improve it? How does your best piece differ from your least effective piece? Like seasoned writers, they wrote of their surprise, their pride in their progress, and how their view of writing changed.

For the final exam I asked them to compile a portrait of themselves as readers and writers. With their drafts, final pieces, assessments, and logs before them, they were to select three pieces to include in their portfolios and discuss them in a letter of introduction to their following year's teacher, "the Reader of My Portfolio."

Laney wrote,

To the Reader of My Portfolio,

You are entering another dimension, a dimension in which echoes of memories of the buried past—the past that lives beneath your fingernails and fades into the omnipresent shadows—are the cold, eerie, underlying chants of the alter—future, and alterpresent. You are entering Laney's world, MY WORLD . . . and there is no going back. This sensation will always live under your skin.

In my life I believe I was always a writer. I have no single favorite author. I embrace all styles and forms of writing, and I take a little from each of them. . . .

I used to think writing was like painting a picture with words, mingling different tones, shades, and textures; merging them and pulling them until on their own level, without me, they connected. But what I realize now is that writing is much deeper than this. Writing is the second creation. Writing is sharing in the creative act and I have become a slave to recording it. . . .

"Bus" came to me while I was riding the bus. I was half asleep, half brain dead when suddenly an unveiling. I scrambled for pen and paper and wrote and wrote. I worked and reworked it and even now it can use another draft. Perhaps my transition was too abrupt. I chose this piece to show my descriptive skills.

Ah, "Blind." This may be the best piece of writing that I have done all year. In this, I really tried to show not tell what was happening.

The last line came to me before I went to sleep one night, so I wrote it down. (This is not an odd occurrence. I have become accustomed to keeping a pen and paper by my bed.) The next morning I looked at it and beyond it. In a flash I saw the story like I see all of my stories—revealed. So, I wrote it and you read and feel it.

I cannot say that any of my pieces are actually complete. . . . To be honest, I think I will be reworking until the day I die.

"Plastic Agony Mass-Produced" was a new idea for me to try—poetry. I really have never written poetry, I am a prose-girl. It seemed though, that when I got the idea for it, it had to be poetry. Poetry does not come to me the same way prose does. This is my creation. . . . The form, I am afraid, is weak. . . .

I learned things about myself from writing just as I learned things about writing—mainly that I will never be able to disconnect myself from it and that it is one of the most beautiful forms of art in the world.

Reading a book is entering another's dimension. Ayn Rand has a good foreword about reading in The Fountainhead, *but I can't recount it now. I read fifteen books this year and I wouldn't give the experience back for anything. I would have read more but school takes up most of my time. Reading is the single most important human function besides eating and breathing.*

The beauty of extended periods for writing and reading is exemplified in Laney's response. Careful selection and rearrangement of the curriculum can allow most students time to write on their own.

In her final assessment, Kathy wrote,

> *As I look back on how much I wrote this year, I am very proud of myself. . . . Writing is like smelling a flower. Some flowers are sweet and fragrant and you want to smell it more. Others have absolutely no fragrance or smell bad and those are the ones that need revision or to be thrown out.*
>
> *I chose "The First Day" because after five drafts I thought I satisfactorily thought like my Dad did on his first day of high school. My strengths for this piece are my introduction and attention to detail. To improve this, perhaps I could go into even more detail or make it one big metaphor. . . .*

Kathy discussed two more pieces and continued,

> *Reading a book is like eating an apple. Once you break the skin, you can't stop! This year I read a total of ten books. I am very proud of myself because before I wasn't a big reader, but since you allowed us to read whatever we wanted, I read. I noticed too that my vocabulary grew. When writing I used a word and a few times I had to look it up to know what it meant. How did I learn it? It must have slipped in from one of my novels. . . .*

Alisha compared last year's writing to this year's:

> *Looking back on my writing from last year I feel that my writing skills have blossomed as a sophomore. In previous years, I considered writing and reading a drag but this year I have been encouraged to look at writing and reading in a*

different, creative way. The main focus wasn't on spelling, punctuation, or grammar but on the content of the paper and I appreciate that. Writing is no longer a drag. I look at my world as endless possibilities of stories. An open drawer, spilled milk, a pair of glasses on the counter are seeds for stories. . . .

Reading is like lying on your back in a big, open field on a cloudy day. One cloud takes the form of the dog next door, Aunt Gertrude, an ice cream cone, and a frog prince looking for his princess' kiss. Reading takes us places we could only dream of going to and meeting people we wish were our best friends. I read twenty-two books this year! I don't usually read this many books, but I started reading Lurlene McDaniel's series and couldn't stop. By writing weekly logs I was able to make connections between literature and my life as well as make predictions even though not many of mine were right. My favorite book was Don't Die, My Love *by Lurlene McDaniel. I cried through half of it. It makes me realize how precious life is. Reading and writing are closely connected. While reading one can go places and meet new people. While writing you can decide where you or your character will go and whom you will meet. Reading is an adventure already made by another, whereas writing lets you be the first to explore.*

In retrospect, one of the most powerful elements of my program was that knowing the students were in search of identity, I provided time for them to pursue this intensely inward quest through extended time for reading and writing. I now know how to allow the students to write what is meaningful to them, how not to take charge of a student's writing, how to make time for reading, and how to measure student growth. Likewise I learned the power of telling students what they are doing right. I made invaluable exchanges.

Had these students grown as writers and readers? Yes. Learning, though, is difficult to measure. What will they remember? What will they carry with them? It's not for me to say. This I know: they have left a paper trail of what they've thought, felt, and believed. If they found that learning is fun, or that writing is a great release, or that words carry powerful experiences, then I was successful.

CHAPTER 5

"In the End All Books Are Written for Your Friends": Motivating Writing Through Peer Audiences

Cheryl H. Almeda

In a secondary language arts classroom, students are involved in a variety of tasks ranging from reading silently and aloud to taking vocabulary tests to writing on a range of topics. In the past, I liked to believe I was doing the most that could be done: challenging students to share their thoughts in writing on a variety of topics in a variety of ways, and when they had completed the assigned tasks, responding with a grade. Year in and year out, these techniques met with measured success. Students who were very grade-conscious sought to fulfill my requirements for an A, but I sensed that they felt little or no satisfaction in their work, and I witnessed more than a few dumping their papers in the trash after I handed them back. As for the students who remained unmotivated by the grade, their papers became less frequent and lacked the level of quality I knew the kids could achieve. As the year progressed, teacher-student interactions seemed to become less and less important to the students, while interactions between peers became more and more significant. I longed for a way to include peer interactions in classroom writing experiences and anticipated that the results of these experiences would include better papers and more satisfied students. I began to study the results of involving peer audiences in workshop classrooms.

> *Ms. Hernandez's second-graders are preparing for Author's Chair. Before coming to the circle, she asks, "What are some ways we can show we are listening to the author?" She encourages students to tell strategies they have been using— watching the speaker, setting purposes for their own listening, and forming questions as they listen. She lists the suggestions on the board and then adds a new one, blocking distractions. After about five minutes of discussion, the students come to the carpet, where Ms. Hernandez reminds them of today's purpose for Author's Chair: Henry wants comments and questions to help him revise his composition. (Anderson and Brent 1994, 67)*

This familiar setting is a successful one in many elementary classrooms, but I wondered how I could transfer the excitement and motivation to a secondary school classroom.

In describing literacy-rich classrooms, researchers Sulzby, Teale, and Kamberetis comment that teachers in these classrooms "encouraged students to (1) write for ownership, (2) use writing in their play, (3) use writing in response to literature they hear or read, (4) share their writing and respond to other children's writing, and (5) use writing to communicate with other people" (cited in Deford et al. 1993, 111). By providing my students with opportunities to listen, read, speak, and write with each other, I tried to recreate these same kinds of meaningful experiences in my tenth- and twelfth-grade classrooms.

The popular adolescent fiction writer S. E. Hinton once said, "I advise writing to oneself. If you don't want to read it, nobody else is going to read it" (quoted in Murray 1990, 38). Writing for oneself is an ideal place to start, but for highly emotional and relatively insecure adolescents, writing for others is also an important goal. Each of us longs for appreciation and respect from those around us. I agree more directly with the poet Mekeel McBride: "In early drafts, a poem is for me. After that, it's for anyone, everyone" (quoted in Murray 1990, 39).

English 10: Peer Conferring

To begin this process of involving students in each other's writing, I decided to talk about my own writing. On day one in my tenth-grade classroom, we wrote a class book about ourselves and passed each chapter around, searching together for "the seven truths" about each of us and "the three lies." These were just single, silly statements that anyone could have come up with, of course, but now they were ours as a class. On day two, we began a writing workshop, and at the conclusion of the period, I asked if anyone had an error that needed correction or a suggestion on how to improve a paper. No one volunteered, so I stepped in. "Here I sit," I began,

> *the words dance before me*
> *they hover like bees*
> *as I try to bat them away.*
> *Have you ever been stung by an adjective?*
> *Ones like "ugly" or "fat" create the most . . .*

"OK, this is where I need help. How should I finish the line?" They stared at me. "*Us* help *you?*" they seemed to ask. "But you're the teacher."

Then Brooke raised her hand. "How about, 'create the most painful punctuation'?"

"Yes, that's it!" I exclaimed. "Perfect." We all smiled. *Our* poem was perfect.

From here, we moved on together, drafting, revising, and editing. At first many of our interactions dealt with finding topics, and most conversations were between teacher and student. Most writers were hesitant about discussing a friend's writing. "At the beginning of the year, students aren't too helpful as editors since they're often fearful of hurting someone's feelings," says Mark Barber, a language arts teacher in Homewood, Alabama (quoted in Manning and Manning 1994, 60). However, through modeling and repeated peer conferences, the students grew more confident over the next several weeks and were more willing to serve as editors for their peers.

Involving peer editors in the students' writing took some pressure off me, since I could circulate in the classroom instead of feeling the burden of looking at each paper and pointing out obvious errors. "Groups of students read each other's writing three or four times before I even see their papers," explains Guy Doud, a National Teacher of the Year in Minnesota who works within a similar workshop format, "so most of the rough edges—careless thinking and mechanical mistakes—don't even reach my eyes. I reserve my time for raising substantive issues on [their] papers" (quoted in Silberman 1989, 124).

After drafting and peer conferences, the students revised their pieces. Then, in teacher editing conferences, I sat down with each writer one-on-

one and together we focused on the strong and weak points of the paper before us. The students did not receive a grade at this point, only a suggestion or two about how to make their papers stronger before taking them to the final draft stage. Terry Moher, a high school English teacher in Exeter, New Hampshire, suggests that "One idea per conference while students are immersed in the process of writing, is more helpful than ten ideas on a piece that is already completed" (quoted in Silberman 1989, 131).

Other teachers may contend that students will not be motivated to improve their writing unless they receive a grade. Students who have worked in process-oriented classrooms, however, disagree. Brian, a student in Fairfax County, Virginia, observes,

> *If these teachers saw writing as a process, they would understand why our writing has to improve. When you get a grade after it's too late to change anything, you can't find better ways to express yourself. But when you have conferences with teachers and other students as soon as you're ready to show them an early draft, you have time to work through one revision after another. That's what I call "improvement"! (quoted in Silberman 1989, 144)*

This process—writing, conferring, and revising—worked for a variety of topics and structures. At times, we wrote on self-selected topics in self-selected genres and styles. At other times, we wrote with a specific focus in an assigned genre. Peer editing and teacher conferences provided a map through the confusing trails of revision, but I was still faced with the question of how to move the students from rough draft to final copy in a way that was motivating and challenging. If I was to be the only one to enjoy their final pieces of writing, what did it really matter if they were typed or scribbled in pencil, and who really cared if the introductory paragraph included the thesis statement? In the grand scheme of an adolescent's life, I didn't matter much.

Read-Alouds

Introducing read-alouds (oral sharing of writing) solved many of these problems. Because of the diversity of material I needed to cover in my senior and sophomore classes, the structure of the read-aloud varied. In the sophomore class, I scheduled a read-aloud once every six weeks: each stu-

dent read a self-selected piece from his or her portfolio. As a class, we listened and enjoyed one another's work, and responded by snapping our
fingers (clapping was too loud). "Opportunities should be provided for responses by many [students], not just the few who volunteer. [Students]
may be encouraged to tell their answer to a partner or to respond with
hand signals (e.g., thumbs up) or response cards" (Anderson and Brent
69). This kind of communication convinces teens that what they have to
say is important and that someone is listening.

After the first, scary experience, students grew increasingly fond of the
read-alouds and always shared their best work. I discovered that these oc-
casions motivated the students to write carefully and with a wider audience in mind. No longer was my opinion the only one that mattered (or
didn't matter). Now the whole class was experiencing this piece of writing from this particular author, and its reception was important. Sixteen-
year-old Sarah explained that "for a read-aloud, I chose one [piece of writ-
ing] that showed emotions strongly or created a mood [so] as to keep the
audience's attention." Alisa affirmed the importance of read-alouds: "I believe pieces need to be read. . . . Pieces with an intense content need to be
read out loud."

Every language arts teacher wishes her students would take editing
more seriously. This too can be aided by the incentive of a read-aloud. As
Meghan, a sophomore, noted, "I don't normally change my process for a
read-aloud. . . . The only thing I would change is how many times it [my
piece] is edited."

Brooke grew up in a literate environment. With two supportive parents, including a father who is a professional writer himself, Brooke entered my classroom ready to please me and ready to grow as a student.
As the year progressed, however, Brooke's focus shifted from what she
thought I wanted to hear in poems titled "America" and "Lethargic Angel"
to pieces she needed to write. During our second read-aloud session,
Brooke surprised me with a piece I hadn't seen before. It was not written
for me, but for Brooke and her peers of fifteen and sixteen. It spoke to
them most effectively and remained a favorite for both of us.

The Question

> If I were not me and you were not you, would you roll your
> eyes as you impatiently waited for me to fumble with my
> wheels through a door which was too narrow, swinging
> back to clap my "mobile" chair? Would you shake your head

*as I tried to yield but saw that there was no ramp to my ap-
pointment? Would you sigh and glance at your watch as I
looked for an elevator but instead, saw only a mountain of
steps stretched out before me? Would you push past me, not
bothering to assist, and dash toward the stairs to avoid any
further delay?*

*I already know the answer. You wouldn't. In two sim-
ple words: you wouldn't. You know how it feels to be the in-
convenience. You know how it feels to be in need when
everyone around you resents your existence. You know
what their eyes feel like as they burn through the back of
your neck.*

*You know how it feels. I don't know why they stare as
you struggle. I don't know why they sigh as you suffer. I
don't know why they never stop to succor you as you are in
need.*

When she finished "The Question," Brooke was met with a snapping
finger applause and open-mouthed stares. She had made very real those
situations that many of my students confronted every day in our high
school. Brooke did not use a wheelchair, but many students did, and for at
least a moment, we were confronted with the reality of their challenges.

At a later read-aloud, Brooke shared "Time."

*Inside and outside
back and forth
A dodge and a handshake
Hi. How are you?
Fine. How are you?
Empty smiles
Busy miles
Too much to do
Places to go
Never stop and
Get behind
Lose the game
of Time.
With no reward
only more work
And a busier day*

Walk faster
Don't stop and . . .
Hello
Oh no!
I'm late
Good bye
The clock spins faster
So much to do
before the clock
Stops.

Our frantic pace slowed momentarily as we allowed ourselves to enjoy each other's work and appreciate each other's company within our community of writers. This community expanded at the end of the year when the class invited other faculty, parents, and friends to our final read-aloud, complete with candles, cupcakes, and decorations. The audience marked our writing efforts as successful by applauding and purchasing copies of the class anthology students had cooperated in putting together.

English 12: Whole-Class Sharing

In my senior English classroom, the read-aloud took a different form. Due largely to the amount of British literature we were expected to cover, our in-class sharing time was more limited. After prewriting and peer conferencing on rough drafts, I asked five students to volunteer to share their pieces in a whole-class workshop. The old Chinese adage rang true: "Tell me and I forget. Show me and I remember. Involve me and I understand" (quoted in Trelease 1989, 46).

Chad, one of the volunteers, reacted to his experience in the workshop this way: "I took more time because I knew my peers would be reading [my paper] as well as my teacher [and] I want my peers to think I'm a good writer." Each student was required to participate once during the year. The read-aloud covered topics and genres I had assigned and it was anonymous: I made copies of each piece for the class; we read them silently to ourselves and then commented orally with remarks both critical and congratulatory. The five authors sat among us, taking notes and listening to our reactions. After the whole-class workshop, the five took their pieces of writing through a third stage with further revisions.

The students found the experience helpful. William observed, "I find writing workshop causes me to think about my writing a little more. I tend to think about misspellings, word usage, and punctuation whereas if I was just doing a regular essay, I would worry far less about some of these things." Katie gave a good reason for such care: "I took into consideration all of the comments that my classmates had made about other papers, making sure I didn't repeat those mistakes. In writing workshop, it's sort of like you have to prove yourself to your classmates." Shahana agreed, saying she liked "the challenge of trying to make my paper so good that nobody will make any negative comments." Carrie agreed: "I feel that I do tend to try to perfect my paper and make it the best I can when my peers are going to read it."

Molly said she "notice[d] when I was writing for the workshop I was more careful with spelling and the words I chose, since I was going to be in the spotlight." Every teacher wants a student to experience "the spotlight"; these are the moments the students take with them. Paula seemed to summarize a general truth when she wrote, "The more who read [my writing] the better I try to do." At the end of the year, I asked the students to choose their favorite pieces of writing, and they consistently selected the workshop pieces. These mattered most because the audience mattered.

Other Ways to Share

The writing workshop is not the only place where the audience matters for young writers. Informal sharing helps to create camaraderie among students and adds value to each student's response.

Journal Pair-Shares

For several years, journals have been recognized as an effective way to encourage writing about literature and further discussion. But I have found that even the most motivated students lose interest in freewriting as the year progresses. "How long does it have to be?" and "Are you really going to read this?" begin to crop up in discussion more and more frequently. Asking students to share their journal entries with another student ("pair-share") expanded the audience, and students' interest in good writing increased. A typical pair-share might involve turning to the person in front of or behind and reading to that neighbor. Or it might involve selecting a favorite line from one's own work or a partner's and highlighting or circling it. After a while, students began sharing their writing aloud with the rest of the class.

"Best of Row" Competitions

In the past, when I assigned poetry I set up a few guidelines but mostly just encouraged the students to give each assignment a satisfactory effort. While this was enough motivation for a few, for most it meant an evening that didn't include English homework until the bitter end, when they dashed something off. "Best of Row" competitions put the fire back into these dying embers. When my British literature seniors brought in original poems, they met with the other members of their row to share their poems and select the best one. I read the row winners aloud to the class and we voted for a class winner. (A row could not vote for its own entry.) Writing poetry became akin to a team sport. Individuals were rewarded for their poems, but the entire winning row also benefited from their selection; the quietest, most thoughtful student could be elevated in status by bringing home a victory for his teammates. "BOR" competitions proved to be simple yet highly effective practices for improving the quality of poetry assignments.

Poetry Presentations

Poetry presentations gave students the chance to choose a poet for further study. On an assigned Thursday, each student took ten to twenty minutes of class time to share some background information on the poet and some of his or her poetry. The only requirement was that the student must engage the class in the study of this poet and poetry in some way. The presentations in my sophomore class were outstanding. Literary artists chosen ranged from Dylan Thomas, e.e. cummings, and Shel Silverstein to Lewis Carroll and Jim Morrison. Several students made delicious "poem" desserts to share with the class (for example, one student frosted one word on several cupcakes then arranged the cupcakes to form a poem), some led us through color-marked overhead transparencies identifying metaphors and points of alliteration, and others led us in charades to discover the titles of several of Walt Whitman's works. I gave no grades for these presentations. It was not my opinion, noted in my grade book, that mattered to these students; instead, it was the all-important audience reaction that inspired them and motivated them to go above and beyond what was "required."

"When I'm writing I'm always aware that this friend is going to like this, or another friend is going to like that paragraph or chapter, always thinking of specific people. In the end all books are written for your friends." This observation, from Gabriel Garcia Marquez, suggests that the writer in each of us longs for an audience that will support us and approve what we write—one we care about. I have come to realize that I am not always the best audience for my students. By nurturing informal sharing, workshop and read-alouds within our classrooms, we can motivate students to write more carefully by writing for each other.

CHAPTER 6

My Search for Reflective, Thoughtful Responses to Reading

Debra Ciambro Grisso

Minilesson #1: Starting the Process

"Then we ask ourselves, 'What is the one thing I can suggest or demonstrate that might help the most?'" (Calkins 1994, 194). As Lucy Calkins so simply states, in teaching we search for the best, most productive way to make ourselves understood. For me that way has been the minilesson. When I implemented the reading and writing workshop in my eighth-grade classroom, I created minilessons to replace my lengthy lectures. One topic I addressed repeatedly was journal writing, since this task proved to be difficult for some students. Over the course of an entire year, I struggled to elicit from my students thoughtful, reflective journal responses to their reading using minilessons. This proved to be one of the most trying, yet ultimately most satisfying lessons of my teaching career. Saying "It doesn't work" and retreating to safer, more familiar ground would have been easier, but I stubbornly struggled on, somehow certain that my struggle would be worth it. It was.

Journals, logs, and reader responses are defined differently by different teachers. For my purposes, a *journal* is a "way for readers to think using writing, reacting as readers do to any piece of literature or text" (Strickland and Strickland 1993, 116). In our classroom, we call the notebooks in which students write their literature logs ("lit logs" for short). They are housed in the room unless a student specifically asks to take one home. Their purpose is to provide a place for students to respond to their reading in any way they wish: they can draw; write a poem; write a letter to the au-

67

thor, a character, or me; or respond in prose. I define *responding* as telling me their reaction or thoughts when they have finished their reading.

During the first minilesson I gave the students the following list. I believed that providing this list of ideas would make lit logs easy, clear, and manageable:

Suggestions for Reading Responses on Lit Log

I can't really understand . . .

I realized . . .

If I were _____ in this chapter/story, I would/wouldn't have . . .

I was surprised . . .

I know the feeling . . .

I like/didn't like the way . . .

I began to think of . . .

One thing I've noticed about the author's style is . . .

The action is very realistic/unrealistic because . . .

The character's action reminded me of when . . .

This story does not interest me because . . .

I really admire _____ in this story because . . .

The setting reminds me of . . .

The line "_____" made me think of . . .

The character of _____ reminds me of myself when . . .

The character of _____ seems to be a stereotype because . . .

The character of _____ reminds me of someone I know . . .

You may react in any way you wish. These are merely suggestions in case you are stuck. Do not write on this paper, but use it as a help in your lit log whenever you wish.

"In our schools, students often tell us they don't want to write. But they need not bother to tell us," Calkins observes. "We feel their resistance as they eke out tense, tight lines of words and as they ask, "How long does it have to be? . . . Do we have to write? . . . I have nothing to say" (11). Again, Calkins's words ring true. We have all heard these questions. During the first week of using lit logs, I read responses like these:

"In this story their was an old man and a younger man that lived together and the younger one was a maid for the older man because he was crazy" (Pete, responding to Poe's "The Tell-Tale Heart").

"It was stupid because it was boering and I just didn't like it. The begining was stupid and the end was stupid" (Allen, responding to de Maupassant's "The Necklace").

"Boring, good ending. I didn't like the title, too short" (Mike, also responding to "The Necklace").

I did not want to spend the year reading one- and two-line comments about how boring or stupid a selection was; they say absolutely nothing.

It is important to note that some students shared their honest reactions:

> *The other night I watch THE MAN WITHOUT A FACE for the first time. It moved me so much, I began to cry, (Which I had never done before because I thought it wouldn't be 'like a man') I don't know if I ever will again but I just couldn't have kepted it bottle up inside.*
> —Mark (in a response to a television show; students could respond to one each month, if they so chose)

> *I liked this story the most of all the stories we heard last week. I didn't like how greedy Matilda was. I also didn't like how badly she treated her husband. I think she got what she deserved. I really liked the surprise ending! Matilda should have told the truth in the first place and she wouldn't have had to go through all this trouble.*
> —Kathy (responding to "The Necklace")

Tammy responded to the same story this way:

> *"The Necklace" story was a pretty good story. Personally, I would have just admitted I had lost it rather than working ten years trying to pay it off. I would figure that since she had so much money, she could easily buy a new one. I think a lesson to be learned from this story is to admit when you are wrong or when you have done something wrong, because if you try to cover it up, you'll probably work a lot harder than if you just admit it. In the beginning of the story, I didn't like Matilda. She seemed sort of greedy. First she had to have a dress, then she had to have jewels. And she would whine and cry about it, always wishing she had more. Like a spoiled brat. Overall the story was all right. I would probably recommend it to someone.*

After several informal discussions with my students I realized that some of them had never had much opportunity to react to anything. Often their only communication with the teacher had been filling in the circles on multiple choice tests. This kind of writing was a new challenge, and one that seemed to frighten and intimidate some of them. I tried to encourage them by writing positive notes in their lit logs, by not grading mechanics, and by trying through my comments to convey to them how much I wanted to know what they thought as they read. Yet they seemed to have no sincere response: their attempts were painfully weak. I realized that I wanted to see if students who didn't write for the love of it, who weren't strong writers, and who disliked writing could improve in the informal context of the lit log if they received minilessons on writing such responses. I decided to follow six students through the year: three underachievers in language arts, Pete, Allen and Mike; and three high achievers, Tammy, Kathy, and Mark. My goal was to track their progress in writing responses after each minilesson.

My own teaching philosophy demanded that I be a positive role model: I must show the value of responding to what we read. I remembered Calkins's warning against conveying these messages: "It's just five minutes . . . Spelling won't count . . . Just put down anything . . . No one will read it" (1994, 11).

By paying attention to these "guidelines," she suggests, students will never know the thrill and the intimacy of being heard through their writing or the joy of searching and digging, because five minutes precludes sustained thought and meaningful work. Those messages convey the teacher's feeling that writing *is* something to complain about.

I was careful not to introduce the lit logs in this way. Instead, I tried to convey the joy and excitement in really examining and dissecting what we read. I thought they would be encouraged to tell me exactly what they thought. Strickland and Strickland say that "if students are going to think on paper, ideas must be respected and risk taking encouraged. Teachers would do well to avoid grading journals, in the sense of evaluating them for content; however, . . . teachers may wish to assign points for completion" (115). I thought that my positive little notes in their lit logs would nudge and encourage them to tell me more, that they would learn to feel safe and within that safety dig deep into their emotions. I was in for a surprise.

Minilesson #2: Narrowing the Focus

Given the weak responses to the first set of prompts, I decided in the next lit log minilesson to narrow the options. Perhaps the choices were too overwhelming. I asked them to illustrate, explain, or change something in response to a quote from a popular rock song: "emptiness is loneliness, and loneliness is cleanliness, and cleanliness is godliness, and god is empty just like me" (Smashing Pumpkins). I told them that I did not necessarily agree with this statement, even if I could figure out what it meant. I was just asking them to take fifteen minutes to write about it in their lit logs. Once again, the nonwriters responded with less enthusiasm than I expected. They very much wanted to talk about it, but they did not want to write about it. "Do we have to?" and "How much is it worth?" echoed through the room. I was not pleased with what I heard, nor with what I later read.

> "I think it means that being lonely sucks and that if you don't have friends
>   life is dumb."—Allen
> "It's the circle of life."—Pete
> "I don't get it."—Mike

These boys had jotted down these instantaneous thoughts so they could close their lit logs and sleep or play. I went to each, opened their logs, and encouraged them to look closer, not to give up so fast. I even gave each boy some examples of what I meant. They nodded patiently and stared at their logs as if searching for clues. Nothing changed.

Along with the thoughtless nonresponse, there was the ever-present summary. We had briefly discussed the difference between a summary and a response, but obviously not thoroughly or clearly enough. On a subsequent response day, these were two of the summaries:

"Travis helped around the house also. And the hunting and the family. Travis had a dog named Old Yeller. His brothers name was Arliss . . . The little girls name that helped Travis was Elizabeth she was quiet and shy."—Allen

"Ichabod Crane is a very honest person. He came from Connecticut to Sleepy Hollow to be a school master. When he got there people warned him about the spooks and ghosts. He figured out the mystery of the headless horse man and got to marry Catrina who he wished to."—Pete

My students' summaries echoed those Linda Rief received in her classes: "They seemed to be trying to prove to me they had read the books" (1992, 54). I knew it was time to regroup. Although students like Mark, Tammy, and Kathy responded with vigor, there were more who did not. I could not give up on lit logs; I truly saw lifelong value in being able to analyze and express ideas. I needed help. I read more about journals and came across this line in Atwell's *In the Middle:* "Nothing I'd told kids about the letters had nearly the same effect as their reading other students' words—now they could see what I meant" (1987, 201). Rief also told of giving students examples of responses written by students in previous years. Of course! I had modeled peer editing, I had modeled brainstorming, strong leads, satisfying closures; why had I not modeled lit logs? And so I developed another minilesson.

Minilesson #3: Modeling

Once I had decided that my students needed models, I scheduled a minilesson for the beginning of November. November may seem too far into the year for this necessary lesson, but I was also working hard to create minilessons for writing workshop, holding individual conferences on pieces that had gone through the process, providing class time for reading, and doing oral reading of children's books as springboards for minilessons.

In this minilesson we would all read for twenty minutes. I would then go to the board and write my reaction to what I had just read. I had been reading Lois Lowry's *The Giver,* and responding was not difficult: my emotions were close to the surface. When I finished, I read my words aloud. We discussed how this statement differed from a summary, and students seemed to understand. For fifteen minutes, they wrote. I was sure this was just the clarity they needed and waited, eager to read their responses. Pete wrote, "I am almost done with the book I love the way Lynn Banks writes. When I am done I might read Return of the Injun in the cupored." Allen's response consisted of two sentences: "I decided to read a skateboard magazine. It was cool and stuff." And Mike wrote, "I read about five pages. They were cool. I like this author."

I was devastated. These three had made few if any changes and their writing showed little development. The three high-achieving students' comments were as mature and developed as usual. At this point, I was beginning to think that no matter what I did, those who liked writing would continue to put themselves into their writing and those whose attitude about writing was negative by eighth grade would continue to avoid putting out any effort. But I was not ready to give up. I planned a fourth minilesson.

Minilesson #4: More Structure

In my next attempt, at the end of November, I decided that struggling students might need a more structured beginning. Perhaps that would eliminate the screams of "I don't know how to start, I don't know what you want, I don't get it!" I distributed a handout that was to be glued inside their lit logs, a simple list of possible opening lines to help the reluctant writer begin. I made it clear that no one had to use any of my openers; they were only suggestions for when they felt stuck. After our reading, Pete wrote, "The setting reminded me of my brother and the girl he liked, when we lived in Dayton and went to Corpus Christi. It all happened real quick. My brother told me that a new girl came into school and from then on I knew he liked her. . . ." Pete went on for an entire page, filling me in on the details of his brother's situation and how similar it was to the story he had read. I was pleased.

Allen did not write at length but his response was genuine and heart-felt. "I didn't like the way that all those dogs are going to be killed because of lazy people just can't take care of them. If everybody would do what they should and be more resposable pets wouldn't sufer." I knew he was telling me that his reading made him angry, that he saw it as real life "stuff." Again, I was pleased.

Mike wrote, "I realized this story isn't realistic in the 90s, I didn't like it when the chain broke because you can't break a chain trying to take it apart unless it is ten or more years old. That made me not like those parts, except I did like the part in church when they were hitting each other. That part seemed realistic. I realized that some writers probably aren't re-alistic." I had not heard this much from Mike all year. All three reluctant writers responded well when given the chance to use these openers, or prompts. I planned to remind them of this suggestion from time to time throughout the year. The achieving writers I was tracking did not use the suggestions; they didn't need them.

Minilesson #5: Good Responses and Bad

In January I devised a minilesson using overheads to show examples of a weak response and a strong response. This would be different from the last minilesson in that I would compare a poor response with a good one. We read the weak response together and discussed the missing elements: emotion; "I" statements; signs of analysis; and comparison to other writing or to life. Then I put the well-developed response on the overhead and dis-tributed a copy to each student. I asked them to use highlighters to mark evidence of thoughtful responses. They seemed to enjoy this and raised their hands frequently to tell me what they had found. A great discussion followed, and I felt they were ready to respond to what they had read be-fore the minilesson.

Allen wrote about a section of *To Kill a Mockingbird*: "Burros Ellis is a mean, dirty person who dosn't like the teacher. Scout had a very experienced first day. I wonder if every day is going to be the same way for Scout. The teacher should be glad cause she can read and stuff. Dosn't make any since to get in trubel for the good stuff you can do." I was thrilled. Once again, Allen was attempting to express his reaction to the reading. It was honest, it took him more than thirty seconds, and I actually saw him thinking as he was writing!

On to Pete and Mike, who also read *Mockingbird*. Pete wrote,

> *They are saying to walk in someone else's shoes to see how they feel. Because you might not want to hurt someone's feelings and you'll never know what they are feeling inside until you live in their skin, as Addicus said. It is probably hard to find out what other people feel. but if your not for sure how they feel don't make it worse. If somebody gets hurt you may want to walk in their shoes to see how they are feeling so you can stick up for him/her.*

Mike wrote,

> *Atticus says you should get in someone else's skin. the world would be different for awhile until everybody got used to the other person's situation, and then everybody would be in the same situation again, racism and prejudice would start all over again. This would be hard because you can't change your color, religion, or were you come from. I don't ever think we could follow Atticus's advice because we just won't trade places like that. I think the theme of this chapter is you don't judge someone because their different.*

The better-achieving students continued to write thoughtful responses. This one is from Tammy:

> *The world would be a better place if everyone thought like Atticus. His attitude is pure, honest and good. We would know how other people feel and understand people who are so different from us. This is hard to do because we want to put the blame on someone else. No one really wants to understand what everyone else is going through. People put*

others down to make themselves feel better, but don't think the other people are thinking or feeling. We should all follow this advice, wherever we are, no matter what happens to you or others.

My plan seemed to be working. The question that remained was whether or not the students' progress was evident only after minilessons based on concrete, specific models; would they respond so well on other days, too?

Minilesson #6: The Solution . . . "Write Me a Letter!"

Students continued writing in their lit logs through January and February on an average of twice a week. Some students opted to write more frequently, while others went nowhere near the logs unless required to do so. The low achievers had not found their wings or discovered a love for written expression, though the high achievers had done that and wanted to write more and more. The average students seemed to enjoy the lit logs more each month. They were more at ease and more willing to share their thoughts.

At this point, March, spring was getting near, the end was in sight and I still had what felt like a million minilessons, stories, and a novel to finish. How would we ever find time for students to do all I'd wanted them to do? Even with these fears in the forefront, I decided the low achievers were not as successful as they could be with reader responses. I went back to Rief's *Seeking Diversity* for more information, a possible suggestion I had missed or forgotten. I found: "Readers want response to what they write. They want that response to be a dialogue—a confirmation of what they know in a conversational tone" (55).

Perhaps this was where my students felt a void. I had been responding in their logs with brief, encouraging notes, but these were largely evaluative in nature. I had not treated their responses as conversations that deserved conversational responses. Low achievers so often clamor for attention, usually in a negative way. Perhaps this very personal line to me would be something to motivate them. I was right. I provided a minilesson on dialogue responses for lit logs. At least once a week, I said, they had to write a letter to me to tell me how they were responding to their novel. They were free to use any of the openers I had provided earlier, their list of ideas, or any other devices they had learned. The only stipulation was that they had to write to me, and I would read their letters and write back.

The response was positive and long-lasting. We exchanged several letters before the end of the year and each time I was pleased, even with my three "I-hate-writing" boys. I decided that during the following school year, the reading response journals (lit logs) would be composed of dialogue responses.

Given the information I gathered, I believe students who enjoy writing will continue to enjoy it and grow. Those who don't will respond if I take the time to exchange personal letters. For example:

> Dear Mrs. Grisso,
>
> I think reading is OK and all, but this book To Kill a Mockingbird is really boring. There's no point in this book but learning about a bunch of hicks that live in Maycomb County. there has been some good parts in the book such as when Jem lost his pants at Boo Radley's house and had to get them in the middle of the night when Boo was supposedly waiting for a black person. Oh, and I absolutely hate when you use the word Nigger. That sounds like the worst name you could call someone with dark skin. I'd like to tell Harper Lee that.
>
> Sincerely,
> Pete

There had been days, early in the year, when I never thought Pete would express so much of himself to me. Now answering his letters was actually enjoyable. The most difficult part was reacting appropriately when I disagreed so strongly! He didn't like *To Kill a Mockingbird?* My all time favorite? Well, how wonderful that he felt free to tell me that, and that we were communicating about books.

My Lesson: The Power of Correspondence

Once the year was over, I realized that the minilessons were necessary not only for the students to get as far as they did but for me to discover the element I needed the most: dialogue. I still use all the minilessons as the need arises, but we learn to engage in dialogue first. Students write me a letter in their lit logs at least once a week. I answer back at length. My students need the specifics of the minilessons, but they also need constant feedback and audience response. Atwell is right when she says that "opportunities to respond, to engage in literary talk with the teacher are crucial" (164).

All reading teachers worry about the logistics of one-on-one book conferences. They seem to allow little more than a quick synopsis. By responding to one letter a week from each child and staggering the due dates, I made the task manageable. I want to read and respond to five to ten letters per night, not eighty letters every weekend. Atwell's suggestion that students write to other students is another technique for lightening the paper load while keeping a dialogue about books alive and thriving; by counting these letters as well as those written to her as one-third of the reading grade, she maintains accountability (186–195).

As I review my year's trials, failures, and successes, I realize the importance of my journey. Patience, reflection, experimentation, and endurance are everything in teacher growth. It doesn't matter that the experts said it would work; it wasn't working for me until I made it work. Along the way, I learned to value my students' responses. I now know with certainty that they can make a positive connection with reading.

CHAPTER 7

Falling Off the Skateboard: Experimenting with Peer Conferences

Richard D. Hughes

The room had cleared for the day. It was quiet. I dropped Meat Loaf's "Bat Out of Hell II" into the cassette player and fell back into my chair, ready to "shut out the day and make my rock and roll dreams come through" once again (Meat). A voice from the door brought me back to reality.

"Rough day, Ric?" It was Cathy, my colleague, my friend, my sanity at Brown Middle. Meat Loaf was her escape, too.

"Just Randy," I replied. "He sabotaged his conference group again today. I've tried everything I can think of, but nothing seems to be working with him."

She'd heard this story before. "You've tried *everything?* So quit trying. Maybe it's time to turn the kids loose on him," she said as her hand dropped onto the cassette player, abruptly silencing Meat Loaf's wail.

To explain how I reached this point, where Cathy's solution to my problem was right on the money, I have to begin somewhat earlier.

I had initiated my quest to improve my language arts program several years ago by implementing a workshop format based on Nancie Atwell's model in *In the Middle.* My students enjoyed choosing their own independent reading material and responding to their reading in literature journals. I saw adequate growth, but something was missing, the opportunity to really talk about books and writing and writers.

I had been introduced to the concepts of literature circles and cooperative learning at a National Center for Innovation symposium in Houston in

1991. Literature circles—groups of three to eight students who have read the same story or novel gather together to discuss their reading—sounded good. They were student-led and encouraged students to talk and to question one another in ways that just didn't seem possible in a whole-class discussion orchestrated by the teacher. I thought this was the missing ingredient and immediately set about making the groups a permanent part of my curriculum. As my classes and I experimented, however, I found the noise and confusion of twenty-eight middle school bodies all "chatting literature" at the same time in a confined area overwhelming. As a result, I filed these "cooperating" group activities away "for future reference." Some self-selection of reading materials and an occasional free-choice writing assignment again became the norm.

In the years since then, though, I have come to realize the importance of turning ownership of students' learning over to them. Peer and group conferencing became a necessity. But how could I comfortably make these activities a part of my classroom? Something would have to change, and I knew that I needed to change the most. The problem in my classroom was not confusion and the noise, it was my need to control the students' learning process.

As I've learned during my teaching career, it is much too easy for a teacher, standing in front of a captive audience of hormones in tennis shoes, to fall into windy explanations and lectures. Too many voices in these classrooms go unheard. In a workshop setting, a truly successful teacher strives to become unnecessary. Group conferences provide a forum for unheard voices to be accepted and valued. I started over, more slowly this time.

In many ways my students became the subjects of my experimentation and research. I was straight with them from the start.

"You mean guinea pigs?" Emily shouted from the back of the room that first day.

"How long have you been teaching?" Michael groaned.

"My mom talked to the guidance counselor and got my schedule changed because she wanted me to have you this year, Mr. Hughes, and now you're changing things. I don't think she's going to like this," Emily added.

Twenty years of working with middle school students had prepared me for these reactions. "I suppose it would be too much to ask you to freeze where you are for two years. You see, I've learned some awesome things about teaching writing, but I know I'm never really good at something until I've worked through it and practiced it for about two years. Two years from now I'll know better what I'm doing. Right now you and I are going to have to stumble our way through and hope for the best."

There. My confession was complete. After a good sixty seconds of quiet (definitely a record for any eighth-grade classroom), Michael again broke the silence.

"C'mon, guys. It can't be that bad. We don't have textbooks in here."

Discipline, Control, and Boundaries

Change forces self-examination. I wasn't about to throw out philosophies of successful teaching I had believed in for some twenty years. But how did this workshop approach fit in with my tried and true methods? What went wrong when I attempted workshops and group conferences? How did these new approaches conflict with what had been engraved on my teacher's heart?

> *THE VERY FIRST AND MOST IMPORTANT STEP TOWARD A CONTROLLED CLASSROOM IS A WELL-PLANNED, MULTI-ASPECT LESSON THAT HAS NUMEROUS RELEVANT AND INSTRUCTIVE EXAMPLES, A LOGICAL AND GENTLE PATH THROUGH THE ABSTRACT CONCEPTS, SOME APPLICATION AND PRACTICE GUIDED BY MODELING, AND A REASON-ABLY HAPPY AND CENTERED TEACHER TO PRESENT IT.*

My past attempts had failed, I realized, because the rise in discipline problems became too frustrating. I was tossed off-center. Turning the classroom over to a group of "undisciplined" thirteen- and fourteen-year-olds without adequate instruction in self-regulated learning had created chaos. Without discipline, even the very best middle school students are basically loud, pushy, silly, mouthy, and at times unusually cruel to each other. They will watch carefully and gleefully enlarge upon any foolish act that goes unstopped.

My attempts to introduce a workshop format, and group conferences specifically, demonstrated that middle school students are neither noble by nature nor filled with the intellectual curiosity middle school philosophers believe they have. Theirs is a sweet picture, but reality is a lot closer to Darwin's "survival of the fittest."

If successful workshops and group conferencing were to become realities in my classroom, my first priority had to be creating that "logical and gentle path" of shared control and responsibility. In establishing an environment that encouraged independent learning and risk-taking, I had to guarantee self-discipline and acceptance to teach and review and model and teach them again. The workshop approach presupposes an environment of trust and cooperation. That doesn't mean turning all control over to the students. In this kind of setting especially, students want the teacher to be in control. Otherwise they would say and do stupid things that embarrass themselves and hurt each other. Classrooms lacking such an arbitrating presence are more like battlefields; the kids know it's war and defend themselves against each other's pranks and taunts. They get little out of the class except cheap entertainment when they aren't the current target. Classrooms like these offer no safety, no advancement, and no feeling of accomplishment. Students have no reason to respect the teacher or themselves. Even more damaging is the unspoken message: nobody will help them; nobody is fighting for them; nobody cares, period.

To avoid that perception I introduced several elements. For the entire first quarter of the year we focused on read-alouds, role-playing, open discussion, freewrites, and daily sharing of one another's writing. My students needed to recognize that in this classroom we valued learning as opposed to performance, individual effort and progress instead of final perfection. It was a slow process, but a most important one in helping students to explore their own ideas while accepting each other's. In order to reach the understanding that risk-taking was applauded and safe we had to establish fair and sensible boundaries. It was OK to pass, without fear of question or judgment, on sharing a piece of writing too personal for others to hear. Students learned to analyze and critique the writing, not the writer. And they learned that I was strong enough, if need be, to protect them from each other and from their own uncontrolled actions.

Ultimately, each student is in control of whether he learns or not. I once thought that because I directed classroom activities, controlled the timetable for learning, decided the methods of instruction, and determined the consequences for my students, that I was in control of the learning that occurred in my classroom. What a big mistake! Students are in charge of their own learning, even though most do not realize it themselves. As I taught classroom procedures, routines, and process writing through a series of minilessons, the students were able to see and believe that they played a major role in their own learning.

By the end of the first quarter, Language Arts Workshop had become a respite from the chaos of the rest of the day for many students. The turmoil of being a teenager among other teenagers and sometimes crazed adults was calm for an hour and a half in this safe place where, if they were at least trying, they'd find encouragement and recognition.

Small-Group Conferences

Our adventure in small-group conferences began when my students and I agreed that we felt safe enough to try it. We spent time discussing and reviewing strategies and techniques that worked well during whole-group sharing of freewrites and drafts. Before moving into conference groups we role-played what might actually happen when four or five writers broke away from the safety of friends and the larger group and attempted to function on their own. So far, so good.

How to group students was a major concern, and the scholarship on the subject was less than helpful: A group that is too large allows less individual participation and provides more opportunity for conflict. There's bound to be a point of diminishing returns (Vacca 1995). Female students relate to other group members and achieve at higher levels depending on the gender mix of the group. Male students seem more likely to compete, while females seem more task-oriented. Female students try to assist their fellow group members by offering suggestions for improvement, while male students more often tender criticism (Dillow, Flach, and Peterman 1994, 49). Allowing groups to remain intact for extended periods establishes collegiality (Gartin and Digby 1993, 11). Group membership should change when a new cooperative learning task is assigned (Johnson and Johnson 1991, 3). Because students know instinctively from whom they can best learn, they should be allowed to choose their own groups (Burton 1995).

Having read and listened to the "experts," I asked my students for their opinions. After all, they were the major stakeholders. Both high- and low-achieving students expressed a strong preference for working in groups. They said that group work helped them generate ideas and provided them a way to get to know other students. "When there's more than just you participating," Candace said, "when it's the teacher participating with you and the students participating with you—anyone participating with you— it becomes interesting because you learn something about that person." The one major objection to group work was raised by high-achieving students who explained that they ended up doing not only their own work but that of the less-motivated students as well.

Keeping in mind that a writing group is a place where members offer each other support and suggestions and that the experience should enable and empower each writer, I tried to structure each group according to a mix of abilities and genders, aiming for four as the ideal number of members. Looking over my list I wondered which groups would work and which ones would not. How much influence would the higher-ability students have on the lower-ability students? Would the latter begin to notice and correct the weaknesses in their writing? Would total chaos return?

From that point on, peer conference groups became a part of our weekly routine. Wednesdays became Peer Group Conference days in addition to our daily writing (which involved prewriting, drafting, peer conferences with another student, self-editing, revising, and a teacher conference). Each week, students were responsible for bringing a new piece of writing. We arranged the desks into groups in the morning; later, once they had secured ditto'ed forms to guide their responses (see Figure 2), one student read his or her writing aloud. The other group members listened and then wrote down their first impressions. During a second reading, group members focused on specifics: what they considered really good about this piece, not so good, and any questions they had. Then, one by one, the listeners shared their reactions and passed their response forms to the writer. We repeated the process (adapted from *Beginning Writing Groups*) until everyone had had a turn. Cut and dried! Simple! No scribbled red marks! No opportunity for conflict since no one ever needed to defend or explain what he or she had written, and it was up to them to decide whether or not they acted on any of the suggestions. As a last task each Wednesday, students recorded their group and individual successes and failures on an index card.

Types of Groups

Over the course of the year, as my students became more comfortable in their "guinea pig" role, I made some interesting discoveries. Three types of groups emerged: those dominated by a leader, those with an unofficial, silently elected leader, and those with no visible leader.

A Group with an Acknowledged Leader

Ian, Pete, David, and Adam created a typical leader-dominated group. Ian had begun the year pretty much an isolate, but gained a reputation as the one who could find and solve just about any writing problem presented to him. He became the most sought-after one-on-one conference partner in the room. Enjoying his newfound popularity, he happily took control of his group, assumed and directed the majority of the workload, and served

Your name _____ Date _____

Author's name _____

Title of piece _____

First Reading: First impressions

Two or more sentences about your emotions/reactions to this piece
(45 seconds)

Second Reading: Be specific!

What you like about this piece of writing:

1.

2.

3.

4.

5.

What you don't like about this piece of writing:

1.

2.

3.

4.

5.

What you don't understand:

as primary motivator and organizer. Ian's role completely satisfied Pete, David, and Adam, since at the time their physical and emotional involvement was fairly limited. They were grouped with the star of the class and welcomed his suggestions to improve their writing while offering little in return. Knowing that group members couldn't advise him on his writing, Ian sought help from other classmates during regular process writing time. Being recognized as a leader, a position he had never before held, was at first fine for Ian, but in his willingness to help so many, he became overloaded and struggled with time limits in his own writing.

Before the end of the year, Ian realized he had to think of himself before turning to those requesting his help. Adam ran into problems with the juvenile authorities and was removed from school. David and Pete, both capable writers, never achieved the writing growth that Ian did. But in helping others, Ian had helped himself.

A Group with an Assumed Leader

According to Pat, Mike, and Laura, there was no question that Kristina would assume the leadership role in their group. She had been the smartest student in class since second grade, and "boy were they lucky they got her!" But Kristina saw no need for a leader and had a difficult time when all eyes turned her way each Wednesday morning. She took pride in her work and became more and more angry as the year progressed. Finally, in January, Kristina declared that she was on strike. She resented her group members for their "lazy stupidity" and me for allowing them to use her. For a period of several weeks the group members sat together silently, each writing alone. Realizing that their grades were dropping rapidly, they began to solve their problem (with the added incentive that if they didn't, they'd do so in a videotaped session with me). Through negotiation, Pat began to give help rather than just take it, Mike gave up his obsession with writing about Satan, and Laura quit "giggling and acting like a cheerleader." During the last quarter of the year this group was one of the most successful: Group dynamics at its finest!

A Leaderless Group

Overall, the most successful group was one with no visible leader. Jenny, Jessi, Jenna, and Melissa accepted equal responsibility. They believed they were there to help each other, and they were willing and able to give, to listen, and to accept. They worked together so well that, for the most part, they continued to do so outside the group.

Regrouping the Groups

By Christmas most groups were working quite well, but some were floundering. Respecting one another as writers seemed to be the main key to group success. Groups that were failing contained students with very different ability levels and strong personalities. As a result, they had failed to develop a group identity; they were individuals forced to sit together. "It's like Rick and I are in a group alone and Randy and Robert don't do anything but annoy us," Holli wrote one day. "Can't Rick and I go to the hall, ALONE?"

Obviously, I needed to reshuffle the deck. In originally organizing the groups, I had tried to make sure all had equal numbers of able and less-able students, hoping that the higher-ability kids would have a positive effect on the others. But now, kids who were making a conscious choice not to learn were interfering with the learning of those who wanted to write. With the help of sociograms I had compiled in September (see Hubbard and Power 1993, 38–43), I restructured some of the groups, this time making sure that in addition to more compatible personalities, each group consisted of students with varying abilities, including some in the middle range.

This reorganization was by far the best move I made all year. In addition to physically separating the lower-ability students by distributing them among all the groups (divide and conquer?), I had effectively paired up the higher-ability students with many of the often ignored mid-level students. Almost immediately I began to see real changes in these kids. Angie, a writer who had always just gotten by, began to thrive. "My new group is so different from my old one," she told me one day during break. "They really care about what I have to say. If I don't have a decent piece of writing to share on Wednesdays I feel like I'm letting them down." While eavesdropping one day I overheard Lori thank her new group for giving her a new direction for a story she was writing. "From then on the words just spilled out of my pen," she told them.

Giving the higher-ability writers the opportunity to work with others who desired to learn and improve their writing was also a good move. Their efforts were not in vain. They were heard. They were empowered. Their writing and communication skills improved tremendously. Surprisingly, they became very protective of their groups, and where before they would *only* work with other higher-ability writers outside the group, they now willingly sought out any respected group member for individual writing conferences.

Randy

Randy chose to disrupt his first group and his new group. (In his defense, I should note that Randy's life was falling apart. Home visits, team conferences, and time with the guidance counselor changed nothing.) Randy would have no writing to share on Wednesdays, would continually interrupt other group members when they read, and took ridicule to the limits. Allowing other group members to take the matter into their own hands, as my perceptive colleague suggested, seemed the best option after a while. Slowly and methodically, Randy's second group built up an argument on why he should no longer be a member of their group; if he was willing to cooperate and take part, however, he was welcome. He chose not to, and the group fired him. Another group, of his own choosing, accepted him but he only lasted three weeks. As the year progressed, Randy bounced from group to group until finally none was willing to accommodate him. He ended up "on textbook" with me, not my wish, but, nevertheless, "doing" language arts.

Falling Off the Skateboard

Group conferencing has been an important step in improving my language arts program and my teaching. It creates an environment where all voices can be heard. It helps connect writing to reading, reading to writing, writing to life. Does it work for all? Maybe, in time, yes. Does it work for most? Definitely!

I remember one hot, sticky afternoon in October, a writing workshop day. "I can't stand it!" Mike shouted at the top of his lungs. "Why do we have to write so much in here?"

"Writers don't write perfectly the first time," I said. "They turn out page after page of whatever is inside of them and then they cut, choose, splice, rework, focus, change, and substitute." I remember also explaining that in order to be able to discern a pattern to mistakes to improve our writing, we need to write a lot. "It sounds strange to need to make mistakes, doesn't it?" I said. "But it's necessary."

"Sure," Mike said. "I make mistakes and then I get corrected and then I get frustrated and then I start hating writing even more!"

"But what do mistakes really mean?" I asked. "You see them as something you should be ashamed of, as a sign that you just can't write, right?"

"Come on, Hughes, make it real," Mike scoffed, his left foot resting on the skateboard he intended to use in his getaway at the end of the day.

"But what if I weren't teaching writing, Mike? What if I were teaching skateboarding instead? OK, stop laughing. When you fall off that skateboard—because we both know you will—what does that tell me, your teacher? Depends, doesn't it? There's a difference between falling off because you were just goofing around and falling off because you were trying something new and you didn't quite have the idea yet. Your ability to handle the new tricks and experiment on your own is going to depend on how well you already know some of the basics. It's also going to depend on how much practice you get with the balancing, foot placement, pushoffs, body twisting, and final landings. No, I'm not going to teach you skateboarding. But what I'm going to have to do for you if I'm going to teach you writing is similar: see your mistakes as a sign that you need more practice in a certain area and provide opportunities for that practice. When you fall off a skateboard, it could be a balance problem, an incorrect pushoff, or unfortunate foot placement when you tried to land. Your mistakes in writing don't mean you can't write, but that you're working on something new, actually pushing yourself to do something harder and better and more complex than before."

It's amazing how true the saying is that "your words come back to haunt you." In recalling my explanation to Mike, I realized that my attempts at mixing abilities through group conferences were very much like riding a skateboard or cranking out a good piece of writing. Mistakes are part of the process, a part of the growth. Just as a piece of writing gets better in process, group conferencing is fine-tuned in process. If I didn't know that in October, I had certainly learned it by June, when Angie wrote her final evaluation of the class: "Wednesday is what helped me the most in this class," she said.

> *Group conferencing gave me an audience I could trust, an audience I could try new things on. I used to think that writing was just like talking—just write down what I would say. But I learned that writing and speaking are different languages. It used to bother me that we were never allowed to talk about or defend our writing in group, why we were never allowed to answer out loud the questions group members had about our writing. I always wanted to explain something they didn't understand. But I think I figured out why you had us do that. If I explained what I meant I'd never fix it in my writing. Writing has to stand by itself. When I talk, the whole world is helping me get my point*

across. My hands draw pictures in the air, my voice gets louder just at the right times. There's no worrying about how to say something—I just keep spitting words out until someone interrupts me or I'm understood. Writing is different. I have to be understood without all those things helping me out. Yep, writing has to stand by itself. Is that right?

Rock and roll heaven, Angie! That's right!

"What About the Kid Who . . . ?": Workshop Teaching and "Difficult" Students

As Sherri Hall observes, workshop teaching cannot guarantee success with every student. "This approach must not be 'romanticized.' It will not save all of the students. It will save some. It will work for many. But it will not work for them all" (Hall n.p.). No method will, including traditional teaching. Often, though, the test of a teaching method comes in how successful it is with students at the fringes—those whose academic, social, or personal lives do not conform to the traditional classroom ideal: students who are willing to learn, to sit quietly for long periods, to work diligently at tasks with no clear or immediate benefit to them; students who live relatively stable lives and can shut out the distractions of emotional pain, physical discomfort, hunger or need; students who can assume independent identities while in the classroom, uninfluenced by peers, romances, love, or hate. For these students, school life can proceed without incident, and if the teachers' methods affect their learning, it is perhaps less than advocates of one method or another believe.

Those others on the fringes, though, can be the bellwether of the success or failure of one's teaching, because they're less likely to get along, go along, even go through the motions. They're the students who, as Sherri notes, seem to "choose to fail" (Hall n.p.). Workshop teaching won't change all of them, but as the essays in this section argue, workshop teaching allows more opportunities for these students to succeed than does traditional teaching. Why?

One way to answer this question is to return to Walter Sikes's principles of change (see pp. 12–14). After all, learning *is* change. That's an obvious statement, but when we speak of how hard it is for teachers to change, we tend to ignore the possibility that the same dynamics may be at work in our students.

Change always generates stress. School is stressful for students whether or not they are successful. Honors students worry about getting A's and scholarships; average students struggle to understand their subjects and worry about tests. On top of the academic stresses are social interactions, dating, following and breaking rules, all the complexities that arise when hundreds of adolescents gather in one building.

People are reluctant to endure discomfort even for the sake of possible gains. When gains, like "getting into a good college" or "getting a good job" or "being a good citizen," are several years into the future, the discomfort involved in participating in school may simply not be worth it, especially to those students who are less mature or more easily distracted by other elements in their lives.

People resist anything they feel is punishment. For the students whom teachers describe as "difficult," this principle may be central. When students misbehave in school, they are punished verbally, with extra work, with suspensions. When they refuse to do their schoolwork, they are punished with bad grades. But when they try their best, work hard to understand or achieve, but fail to understand, do poorly on tests, or give wrong answers in class, the effect is the same as if they hadn't tried at all: they get bad grades, which they see (rightfully, I think) as punishment. How many students decided long before they hit middle school that it was easier not to "do school" and risk failure than to keep working at it—and risk failure anyway?

Participation in setting goals and devising strategies reduces resistance to change. While students in a workshop environment can and do fail, workshop teaching offers students a way out of the cycle of fear and stress that leads them to be unsuccessful in school. Workshop teaching gives students choices: they may choose what to read or write, how long to spend on various projects, whether to work alone or with others, whether to stay in their seats or move around the classroom. These choices are all denied to students in traditional classrooms, and that lack of control over much of their waking lives leads some students to opt out or act up, both of which are, if self-destructive, proven and effective ways of asserting control from toddlerhood on. Workshops give students the opportunity to participate in their learning.

Will switching to workshop teaching transform students? Not likely.

Unless many teachers in the same school system adopt workshop teaching, students will arrive in workshop classes with attitudes and behaviors shaped by years of traditional teaching. Those who have been successful in those classrooms may find themselves disconcertingly at sea in a new environment where the rules by which they've succeeded no longer apply. Those who have a chip on their shoulder won't brush it off on the first day. As the teachers in this volume found, they may change, but their students don't—at least not right away. Students and teachers must learn how to act in workshop classrooms; for some, that means unloading a considerable baggage of attitudes and preconceptions rooted in years of stress, discomfort, and failure. Here the flexibility of the workshop can help students, since it gives them more freedom to test this new system and make changes slowly, at their own pace. *Behavioral change comes in small steps,* Sikes notes, and workshop teaching, with its delayed grading and increased student choice, can give students the time to take those steps slowly, with help from the teacher and one another.

Classroom Research and Workshop Teaching

Sikes's first principle, *You must understand something thoroughly before you try to change it,* comes through especially clearly in these three essays, too. Traditional teaching—as well as traditional school administration as well—may talk about individual students and their needs, but lesson planning is almost always done in terms of "the class." Teachers' lesson plans are supposed to describe what "the class" will be doing and learning on any particular day, and teachers' schedules and ways of talking use "the class" as the basic unit: "I've got three 10th grade classes, an 11th grade honors class, and a senior AP class this year." "My third period class is giving me fits." Teachers talk in terms of "good classes" and "bad classes," and sometimes those generalizations move beyond a single classroom to infect a whole grade; my oldest son's graduating class was labeled "the bad class" in eighth grade, and that label clung to all the students in that class through high school.

Despite its usefulness as a generalization, talking in terms of the "class" is unfair, even pernicious. In any given class of students, a majority may be hard-working, earnest, and willing, while a small, vocal band of pains in the neck may cast a shadow on the whole class. As in other forms of discrimination (defined as making unwarranted assumptions about a group based on the actions of a few), this one is easy to fall into and hard to climb out of. Workshop teaching helps by presuming that each student in a class is shaping the curriculum to his or her own pace, priorities, and needs; lesson plans, class structures, and teacher assessments are designed to address that presumption. Rather than teach to some poorly defined, generalized "middle," workshop teachers structure their teaching lives around the individuals who gather together to make up their classes.

Even that, however, is not necessarily enough. Mary Anne Anderson, Suzanne Theisen, and Theresa McClain found that to teach their students effectively, they had to study them to find out what made certain individuals in their classes behave—or not behave—as they did. Their focus on individual students has altered how they teach every student they encounter, since they have learned to see their students and classrooms differently. This, I've found, is the best reason to do classroom research: it makes teachers aware, in ways they haven't been before, of the dynamics of individual students as they interact in their classrooms.

As the essays in this volume show, the ways in which teachers come to know individual students depends on their individual research interests. Some teachers read student writing to follow the progress of a curricular change or to see whether an assignment sequence is working; others, like the teachers in this section, allow students to take the spotlight. Regardless, they are paying careful, systematic attention to what goes on in their classrooms, following a plan rather than relying on anecdote and impression (which, especially with difficult students, can often be false or misleading). Paying close, sustained attention yields insights and understanding not available in most day-to-day teaching, and the results are obvious: these teachers came to understand their "difficult" students as complex and talented individuals, rather than assuming that what lay on the surface—disruptive behavior, recalcitrance, bizarre dress, and attitudes—adequately showed the sort of students they were. Ultimately, classroom research teaches us in forceful ways what we often give lip service to but neglect in our daily rounds: that every student deserves our respectful attention. And workshop teaching is a better method for teaching English, because every student—from Mary Anne Anderson's Frank and Theresa McClain's three young men to Suzanne Theisen's Tammy and her "auto boys"—has a real opportunity to succeed, to learn.

CHAPTER 8

Frank

Mary Anne Anderson

These words from Mem Fox's *Radical Reflections* were on my mind as I wondered how I'd survive another year of Frank Dunn:

> *Those who write well have more power and therefore have more control over their lives. It seems to me to be a supreme arrogance on our part as teachers not to see that the granting of this power to our students is politically and socially essential. In the end they're powerless without those skills. Their power won't come about without practice, and the practice can't come about without purpose. The hardest thing for me as a teacher is discovering purposes that will excite my students to such an extent that they'll risk the trauma of the writing battle. (Fox 1993, 21)*

With Frank's poor skills, lack of motivation, lethargy—no, I guess hostility would be more accurate—how was I ever going to excite him enough to want to write?

Throughout seventh grade, Frank had been quite open about his dislike for language arts. He had had plenty of company, since most of the students in his English section were either underachievers or just plain uninterested in academics. Unlike most of the others, who would at least try to do what I asked of them, Frank was vocal about his displeasure. There were no books he was interested in reading and certainly no subjects he wanted to write about. He hated every minute he spent in class and liked nothing we did. In fact, at the end of the year he became so disruptive that I'd had to call in his father to talk about his insubordination. He had started

95

to say things like "This is stupid" or "What's the point of writing that?" in front of the other students. He was getting laughs, but he was also undermining my authority. He seemed to be trying to exert some control in a setting in which in every other way he felt powerless.

Frank had a history of sabotaging class activities. He would make comments quietly, but they would focus everyone's attention on him. In seventh grade he was surprised when these actions resulted in demerits; evidently, because he was not loud or belligerent, he had gotten away with this behavior for a long time. When I questioned his former teachers, they admitted they "put up with" his comments. But in junior high, disruptive is disruptive: demerits, detentions, and parent-teacher-principal-student conferences had served as deterrents throughout most of the year. But May seemed to bring out the worst.

After several further incidents of negative remarks and of encouraging other students not to write about "these stupid ideas," the principal called Frank's father to tell him to keep Frank at home for the last two weeks of school. His father came to the school immediately and demanded that Frank stop being a problem or transfer to another school. Frank chose to stay, and he was subdued until the end of the year.

I wondered what eighth grade would be like. I had thought long and hard about what I would do this year, and decided that I was going to relinquish as much control in the classroom as I could. I would let the students decide which pieces of writing to complete for grades, in which genres they would write, and even what the rubrics would be for grading. Although I had been using Nancie Atwell's basic workshop approach, I had also continued to direct a lot of the class writing and topic choice. Both Atwell and Fox promoted memoir and writing from one's own life, and neither advocated much fiction writing for adolescents. My experiences with prompts for fiction writing from such things as Power of the Pen (a writing program for middle school students), however, had been quite successful. Many students enjoyed writing short fictional pieces, and fiction is a useful way to demonstrate many good writing skills. Would this kind of "choice" help Frank? Would giving him control over these things satisfy his need to control what was happening in class?

At best, I expected passive sullenness, since this eighth-grade class as a whole was decidedly cold and unresponsive. The two sections were grouped according to math levels. The "Algebra" group consisted of typically goal- and grade-oriented students driven to earn their A's. The other group had many underachievers. Frank had been grouped with these kids in seventh grade, but this year he was transferred to the "higher" group because of his math skills. Although the kids in this group were almost all intent on achieving, they were not supportive of one another—unless it meant being opposed to teachers. Then they would join forces. But when it came to peer conferences, discussion, or feedback, it was very much every person for him- or herself. It was definitely not cool to be nice in this group. And Frank was a master of cool.

Given this group's attitude, I was less than enthusiastic, and the first two weeks of school only served to reinforce that feeling. Frank was quiet for a few days, but then he started asking questions. "Why do we have to do this?" I would offer a three- or four-minute answer emphasizing the importance of the daily minilesson, brainstorming, or freewriting. After several days of this, however, I'd had enough. I took Frank into the hall for a little chat about his annoying questions and what the point was in what he was doing. I ended the conversation by reminding him that we could always call his father and tell him that Frank had changed his mind and was ready to transfer to another school. Frank decided to stop the questions. He still may have hated what we did, but he suffered largely in silence.

Meanwhile, I kept wondering how to reach him, how to help him improve his writing, reasoning that if he were a competent writer, he could be encouraged to try new things. Unlike seventh grade, where English and reading were separate classes, in eighth grade the language arts class combined the two. Along with trying to give the students more choice in writing, I also let them choose the novels they read, had them meet in groups (at least at the beginning of the year) to discuss their reading, and asked them to complete journal entries after every fifty pages. Frank's reading skills were actually good—he just didn't "want" to read—so I wasn't as concerned about his reading as I was about his writing.

In teaching writing, I followed Kathleen M. Hunzer's advice in "Freedom as Constraint in the Writing Process":

> *Overall, the students told me that having too much freedom to choose their own topics and to create their audiences can negatively affect their writing. A majority of the students said that they can indeed suffer from writing apprehension or block when they are given too much freedom in choosing their topics. . . . The comments offered by these students clearly show that allowing students too much freedom in choosing a topic can be detrimental; therefore, the students responded favorably to the idea of using guidelines in the classroom. (1995, 3)*

I have often witnessed the ineffectiveness of telling students they can write about "anything." Faced with such an assignment, most students (the very same ones who, when assigned a topic, will whine, "Do we *have* to write about that?") beg for a topic or an idea.

Now I presented minilessons, ideas for brief, informal kinds of writing, and a variety of prompts to encourage creativity. These provided seeds or "beginnings" for the students, who were required to engage in these activities but were then free to decide which pieces they wanted to bring to completion for a grade. I hoped that having this freedom would be a positive experience in "ownership" for students. I also hoped that Frank, who seemed to be trying to "control" me with his outbursts, comments, and behavior, would appreciate this, even though his responses to the reading and writing surveys I asked my students to complete indicated that he did not like to engage in either.

Freedom and Distasteful Topics

Focusing on his new freedom to select which of his pieces would be graded, Frank wanted to know if it was all right to write about his favorite subject: violence. One of the benefits of teaching in a parochial school is that I am free to sideline certain topics or themes as taboo. I have made vulgarities and senseless violence off-limits for years, and usually students don't give me a lot of flak about it. They understand that things not condoned by the church won't be condoned in the classroom, and they relinquish such topics. Not Frank. Even though I had addressed the issue several times the previous year, trying to show him that violence was inappropriate in the classroom, Frank maintained that it was the only thing he could think of.

Now, what about this control? I had to say that I still did not want violence or vulgarities, but we talked again about the difference between senseless violence and purposeful violence. Frank decided that perhaps he could work toward a purpose if he really tried. I told him I was confident that there was so much going on in his brain, he wouldn't have any trouble coming up with ideas. "I have lots of ideas; you just won't like them," he said with a hint of a smile on his face—perhaps not a huge breakthrough but still a more civil exchange than I'd ever imagined.

My joy was short-lived. The first piece Frank finished was a response to an art print of Raphael's *St. George and the Dragon*. The first few paragraphs of the story he began to read aloud in class were filled with gratuitous violence. As I walked around the room toward him, Frank turned to a

fresh page. "I'm going to start over," he said. "I forgot about the 'no violence' thing." Wow, I thought, this is really working. The next day I had a
rude awakening. We had been experimenting with peer conferencing in
groups of four. Students made lists of "ten people you can work with,
and four you'd rather not," and after hours of arranging and rearranging
names, I finally came up with groups. It was quite a surprise to me to see
that Frank's name was rarely listed as someone people did not want to
work with. Since he was so negative in class, I assumed that students
wouldn't want to work with him, but evidently he was a lot more agree-
able with his peers than he was with me. (The people who didn't want
him, though, were adamant!)

When Frank read his "St. George" draft aloud to his group, I was standing nearby. At first I was shocked to hear him reading the same violent
draft he had said he was going to change. His listeners laughed at all the
"right" spots and told him it was "cool." But when they had to give him
feedback, they admitted that they didn't "get it." One went so far as to say,
"What's the point? I mean it's funny, but there is no . . . point." I refrained
from acting as if I was eavesdropping, but inside I was cheering. This
group of students was willing to laugh at Frank's story, but they took their
job as listeners seriously and knew I expected sincere evaluations. This
was an unexpected outcome of giving the students more control. Because
they were in charge of the conferences they could give each other the
kind of feedback that might be discounted or ignored if it had come from
me. But peer evaluation and advice they took seriously.

A week later, as he handed in his draft Frank told me that I was going to
love his story. This is odd, I thought. My interest was piqued. When I read
this story I was going to "love," it felt as if Frank was saying, "In your face!"
Yes, he had changed the violent parts, but he had also figured out a way to
irritate me. The story involved conflict resolution techniques we had
struggled to teach the class the previous year when they were being extremely cruel to one another. The story also proclaimed the Christian principles we try to teach in our school, principles Frank had always labeled
"stupid" or "loser." It seemed that what he was saying was, "If you don't
like violence [and his peer group had indicated it didn't work in his story]
but you do like conflict resolution, I'll give you a sappy story that I don't
believe in. That's good enough for you!" I sensed that Frank was frustrated
with his writing and was looking for a way to divert attention away from
his lack of skills. To assert himself he chose to be antagonistic. Still, he
completed the assignment.

I refused to comment on what I thought Frank was trying to do in this story (annoy me and exercise control), but I did respond to the content: nonviolent, decidedly Christian, improved use of dialogue, still some improper sentences and problems with punctuation. "But is it a good story?" he asked. "Well, it does have a basic plot. There is some development of George's personality, but the characters are basically stock characters, and you don't have much in the way of "showing" details. I guess I'd say I see improvement, but you've got some areas to work on." Frank didn't buy it. "It sucks, er . . . stinks. It's stupid." I reiterated my pleasure at the improvements I could see and urged him not to be discouraged, that good writing takes time and lots of revision. But I sensed that he was unhappy with positive feedback. Was it because he tried a nonviolent story and knew it still wasn't good? Or was it because I wasn't upset that he was obviously parroting the conflict resolution techniques in a "stupid" story? I wondered, but I knew it was unwise to ask him a question like that. He didn't want personal questions.

As I continued thinking about what made Frank tick, I remembered that his two older brothers also had had problems in my class. Each of them had wanted to write violent and/or inappropriate pieces, and each had resisted, in varying degrees, writing personal narratives or anything self-analytical. I knew that they'd had family problems; Frank's oldest brother had been diagnosed with bipolar disorder and his mother had died five years ago after a long battle with cancer. Perhaps the reluctance to write personal narrative was a result of this tragedy, or perhaps of the turmoil in the home because of his oldest brother's problems. From past conferences with Frank's father when Frank's middle brother was in junior high, I was aware that the oldest son had been in and out of counseling and treatment for bipolar disorder. According to his father, Frank held his oldest brother in high esteem and tended to have problems at school due to his oldest brother's influence.

At least I could understand why Frank did not want to write about his own experience, but I thought I was addressing the issue in a positive way by letting students choose which pieces of writing to "finish" and which to abandon as rough drafts. I continued to watch Frank as the year went on to see what types of writing he selected for finished pieces. I tried to provide a wide range of prompts to stimulate ideas, and yes, some of them were based on personal experiences.

Frank seemed to delay writing at these times for as long as possible. He never turned in any writing of a personal nature—not even the required self-analytical portfolio selection paper. He would not select a piece for his portfolio and write about why he selected it and what it showed about him as a writer, even if he had to stay in at recess. Still, I felt that, if nothing else, his behavior had improved, and that was good.

As we moved into the second quarter, I became more aware that, although I thought Frank's improved behavior could be attributed to giving him more control over his writing and reading, I also knew his behavior was shaped by his peer group. In "Student-Centered, Not Teacher-Abandoned: Peer Response Groups That Work," Elizabeth Sommers writes about a college class, but her findings translate well to other ages, perhaps moreso considering how many studies have been conducted on the influence of peer groups on adolescents. She says:

> *when we think about peer response groups, we have to realize that removing ourselves from center stage is not going to solve the problems we have as teachers. Even though we're no longer at center stage, some students will be better writers than others, some will be better respondents, some will be more comfortable with student-centered instruction than others. As transcripts have shown me again and again, peer group talk evolves based on students' power, an authority that develops depending on group status, gender roles, communication skills, writing expertise, and personality. (1993, 8)*

The positive influence of this year's peer group on Frank was noticeable. Working all day with a class that was motivated to succeed was beneficial in itself; coupled with peer interaction in conferences, it was amazing. The students might laugh at Frank's writing because it was not going to be acceptable, but their comments focused on real issues of plot or character or subject matter development. I could never have convinced Frank, as the group did, that his obsession with violence was ineffective. This class was interested in getting the best grades they could and could articulate what was wrong with Frank's writing; the previous year's class either didn't have that understanding or didn't care. And what a difference this peer interaction made. Although Frank continued to turn in pieces with violence, I knew he was revising and trying to develop details to improve the story line. He was making progress in sentence structure and punctuation, a difficult task after years of not trying.

Not only that, but Frank started to take the daily "Caught'ya," a brief grammar and usage exercise (Kiester 1993), seriously too. One day he asked why he couldn't remember anything from the "Caught'ya" exercises we did last year. In my experience, I said, people usually remember what is important to them, and maybe he didn't place importance on them last year. (I could have added, "along with half the other kids in the other group"!) Frank just said "Oh," but he did start to improve (in minute increments) and at least looked as if he was paying attention. I have to attribute this effort, too, to the class. Success and good grades were important to this group and they took their work seriously. Frank's attitude began to improve, which causes me to wonder about the efficacy of tracking in English classes. Would more unmotivated students be influenced to succeed if they interacted with motivated students more in class? It's hard to be the only one in the group with a different attitude. On the other hand, it's also hard to be the only motivated member of an unmotivated group.

Frank's attitude toward me also improved. I knew he would probably never like writing, but he stopped being confrontational. He still wrote violent pieces, but he at least tried to frame the violence in some kind of plot. He never developed an interest in memoir or anecdotal life stories, but that's understandable considering his circumstances.

Sandra Stotsky suggests that perhaps teachers have been focusing too heavily on personal writing. As she reports, "Smagorinsky (1986) suggested that it is a single type of writing that may not satisfy the needs of all students. As he noted from his own teaching experience, 'some people like to write about themselves and others do not'" (1995, 765). Obviously Frank did not want to write about himself. At this stage in his life writing was too threatening and he was unwilling to explore his feelings on paper.

Midway through the year I gained another insight about Frank and control. Because he had earned several demerits from the math teacher for inappropriate behavior (evidently he was being as disruptive and argumentative with her as he had been with me in seventh grade), she, Frank's homeroom teacher, and I had a conference with his father. The math teacher described Frank's refusal to work in class and his assertion that math was "stupid." His father suggested that he be allowed to read in class and do his math at home for homework, even if it continued to take him the two hours he was now taking to complete his daily set of problems. Frank wanted to be switched back to the other, easier math section, but neither the teacher nor his father thought that a worthwhile option. I commented that Frank seemed to be exhibiting the same hostile behavior in math this year he had in English last year, and perhaps we needed to find out why. His father immediately asserted that he didn't want to rehash last year, just focus on the present. I replied that maybe it was the same problem resurfacing and it needed to be addressed, but he wanted to move on.

We agreed that Frank would be quiet in math. The conference was nearly over when Frank's homeroom teacher mentioned that he was pushing the limits of the school dress code. (Our students wear uniforms.) I added that Frank's boots were not uniform, and that I had made him remove duct tape from them earlier in the week. His father asked how Frank had responded to that, and I explained that it was a short but pleasant conversation; Frank said they didn't have enough money to buy other shoes, and I replied that I was sure his father would find the money if I called him. At this, his father got up and walked around the room, visibly agitated. In a low, clipped voice he told Frank they would get shoes that evening—and they would be shoes the father would choose. I interjected that our exchange in class was actually kind of joking. I knew, as did everyone else, that Frank could afford new shoes and was only offering a lame excuse. Mr. Dunn reported that he had questioned Frank about the boots and had been assured that they were permissible.

Afterward, it occurred to me that Frank's father exercised control over him in ways that were probably very frustrating. I recalled a conference the previous year in which Mr. Dunn had broken down while talking about his wife and oldest son, and Frank had climbed over a desk to escape. In May, when we'd met to talk about Frank's insubordination, Mr. Dunn had asked me to leave the office while he and Frank decided what to do. Now he was enraged over a comment that seemed inconsequential to me, although I realized there may have been much more to the story.

This power struggle might explain Frank's insistence on what he was going to write, especially since he didn't like to write. This child had experienced family tragedies over which he had no control and had a father who seemed to exert control in ways that were embarrassing to his son. Maybe that's why Frank tried to exert control in his classes.

As the second half of the year went on, I continued to have a good relationship with Frank. Yes, he refused to deliver self-analytical pieces, but I did not call his father. I talked with him to remind him of the consequences of taking a zero, and he still chose to do so. He completed his other assignments and actually conducted the class in a "Caught'ya" one day when I was late. As I entered the room, he told me they had just finished and erased the board. I thanked him for being so responsible, and in an affected suck-up voice he reported that the class had not been cooperative. I could not resist "admonishing" the class over their rudeness when someone was trying to be responsible. There were several snickers, and of course I had my doubts about what Frank actually did, but I much preferred this interaction to those we had had last year.

One activity that gave Frank positive feedback was our reader's theater, for which we scripted picture books and performed them. Frank was part of the group that worked with Tomie de Paolo's *Strega Nona,* and although I have my doubts as to how much he actually contributed to the writing, he did perform the role of "Big Tony" (changing the character's name was his idea) with heretofore unobserved flair. The first group had been lethargic and monotonous in delivery. But when Frank's group performed, Strega Nona began in a scratchy, shrieky falsetto, and Big Tony's deep, slow voice was a perfect counterpoint reminiscent of Luca Brazzi in *The Godfather.* The kids loved it and so did the principal, who stopped in just after they finished but sat down to watch the encore. Having seen Frank's group perform so well, the other groups then perked up and added a little zest to their performances.

Permitting my students to write fiction had good results, so I was happy to see Atwell reevaluate the practice:

> For most of my years in the middle school classroom my advice to writers who aspired to fiction was please don't. Their fiction overwhelmed me. It was so bad I didn't know where to begin by way of response: bereft of plausibility, specificity, theme, coherence, and, especially, characters even remotely convincing or motivated. (1996, 42)

She goes on to say that although schools have focused largely on memoir and real life writing, many students want to write the things they read, and for most adolescents that's fiction. Atwell is now in favor of giving the choice back to students and not steering them away from a genre they are interested in. Students are capable of exceeding our expectations, especially when they have the desire. And for students like Frank, choosing genres may motivate them to be more cooperative.

While I never saw Frank show a desire to improve, or even to try different things, for most of the year I also didn't sense hostility toward me personally, and we actually had several conversations, albeit short ones. During the last week of school I asked Frank if I could interview him if I gave him extra credit, and he agreed. When I asked what he thought his strengths and weaknesses were as a writer, Frank identified handwriting and punctuation as weaknesses. He had trouble with punctuation because he didn't "know how" to punctuate and he really didn't choose to learn. He felt his sentence structure and punctuation were a little better because he "had" to write. He found writing to be annoying because it took too much time.

I asked what I could do that would help motivate him to read or write, and he wanted me to skip the "Caught'ya," even though he said that's what helped him improve his punctuation. He thought it was better to think of his own topics, even though he only finished pieces in response to prompts. Frank did want to get better grades and turned in assignments that were not self-analytical, but he shied away from metacognitive or reflective pieces, perhaps not wanting to think about how or why he did things. He admitted that when he said he couldn't think of things to write, he really didn't want to take the time; he claimed that laziness and lack of desire were the reasons he didn't want to do any of the reflective pieces. His personal experience and previous counseling had made him wary and unwilling to be reflective in the classroom.

Paradoxically, Frank wanted those things he perceived as beneficial to him to be eliminated because he didn't like them. I don't think he was being facetious; he just didn't spend much time analyzing why he felt things. Years of being unsuccessful in language arts, coupled with years of personal problems, had shaped his behavior in ways he was perhaps unaware were based in avoidance. At least in my class the hostile defenses stopped, and he was no longer disruptive.

Although I can't say I was sorry to see the end of the year, I was grateful that the class went as well as it did. There were no major behavioral problems, but the students remained aloof and unresponsive. Frank's writing improved slightly. He did not pass our state's mandatory ninth-grade proficiency test in March, but he didn't expect to. He still perceived himself as a nonwriter. I hesitate to be too analytical about why Frank's attitude was so negative, but it did improve.

I give credit for his improvement to giving up absolute control and to Frank's move into a more academically motivated group. I am left to ponder whether our school's other underachievers, who are now grouped together, would benefit from interaction with other students. If the students were grouped heterogeneously instead of according to math ability (which our school believes reflects overall ability), would they also improve? If adolescents are influenced more by their peers than anyone else—and we know they are—then Frank's story suggests that teachers and schools should draw on peer influence to promote positive attitudes, good behavior, and improved academic performance.

CHAPTER 9

Wrestling with Vocational Writers

Suzanne E. Theisen

> *Dear Mrs. T,*
>
> *I'm sorry but I didn't read a book to write my report. I have no patience when it comes to reading. I think reading a book is a bunch of B.S.. I know I'll never read a story or a book in the future so why start now? I rather write a story then read a book, and you know how I feel about writing stories. If I really really have to read something why can't it be a short story? A really short story about hunting or maybe something scary? I have no time to read. I get up go to Hudson then Stow then right after Stow I go straight to work and by that time it is really late. So next time if I could read something short in class I'll get my true book report done! "promise."*
>
> > *Your favorite,*
> > *Chucky*

My students are vocational students, the ones with leather jackets, bleached blonde hair, glazed over eyes, and rotten attitudes. They smell of cigarette smoke, an odor that will linger in my windowless classroom for hours. By eleventh grade, the time I receive them, they are convinced that they cannot read, cannot write, cannot behave, and are not socially acceptable.

My bulletin boards broadcast messages like "Don't drop out of life, stay in school"; "A baby is a responsibility not a toy"; "Passing the proficiency test is your ticket to the future." Perhaps the best message is the one that reads "You Have the Power!" It is the only one that doesn't predict poor choices.

Each September, even though I was as eager as other teachers to start a new school year, I was filled with a sense of doubt and inadequacy. These feelings grew each year like a festering sore. Over the years I have been encouraged to believe that vocational students need only minimal teaching to carry them through to graduation. This approach will keep them moving through the system, but it will not foster growth or self-improvement.

Over the previous four years, the skill levels of my students appeared uniformly low. There was no apparent reason why I should expect anything but what seemed to be the norm. However, this year I checked the school records and discovered that my vocational classroom was an extremely diverse community. Not all the students had poor competency scores. Reading and writing ability levels for some started at grade 4.2 but for others it soared past 13.6! This was a surprise. Since some of my previous years' students had not yet graduated, I checked their records and found the same diverse profiles: what they seemed to have in common was the *vocational* label. For some reason, most of these students had *learned* that they were supposed to be disruptive, ill-mannered, slow readers, poor test takers, and in general, losers.

These students had been together since about fifth grade. Many had failed junior high together. Several were second year seniors. Most had difficult home lives, and almost all had experienced repeated failures, either in school, at home, or on the job. I recognized the basic characteristics of most of my vocational students. They were reluctant to trust teachers, had had difficulty conforming to the rules and routines of school, felt they were different from regular students, hated school, hated lunch time, had trouble socializing, had short attention spans, were absent a great deal, were convinced they could not write, and in some cases would not read. There were a few exceptions, students who were truly seeking a vocational career by choice. Unfortunately, the exceptions were few and far between.

This year, however, I decided I would not accept the idea that typical vocational students were totally reluctant learners. Instead, I would assume that they were learners who had learned too well how to manipulate the very system that had placed them in this unrewarding track. In the past, these students were told that they were not writers and so, would not attempt to write. Drills and skills, however, were their specialty. For them, English was any lesson that could be distributed in a worksheet and completed in twenty minutes or less. If a teacher tried to introduce a regular lecture or writing class format, these students would flaunt ignorance as their handicap and proceed to disrupt the classroom and dishearten the teacher. The worksheets and limited reading materials were busywork: easy and, more important, quickly done, graded, and forgotten. This year, though, would be different: each student would have daily opportunities to select reading materials, to work in groups with one another, and to write.

Armed with the new philosophy that even reluctant learners can succeed in reading and writing, with many minilessons, and with an in-class library, I began the school year full of questions: Would my ideas work? Would the students accept responsibility if I expected them to? Could I trust them to read and to write, and would they learn and continue to grow? Would I survive? My classroom had a very different appearance. To the usual assortment of posters showing writing hints, the usual messages about staying in school, and pictures of literary figures, I added maps of the world and current events posters with headlines reporting local, national, and world news. I cleared my one and only bulletin board of all announcements and titled it "Current Authors." Here I posted student papers that could be shared and perhaps recommended for the school literary magazine. I drew from my own classroom library for reading assignments. To teach, I used minilessons, novels, short stories, magazines, newspapers, videos, and oral presentations by students, myself, and guest authors. I permitted students to have a voice in how their papers were graded and invited groups of students to develop rubrics for testing. This wasn't going to be a half-hearted trial; it was all or nothing. Rather than stand and lecture, pass out study guides, and collect dittos, I shifted the responsibility of education to them and became a student with them. Dangerous? You bet! I was never so frightened in my life.

By the end of the school year, however, my students were happier, better behaved, and seeking out knowledge on their own. Through their cooperative learning they were becoming experts at working as a team. Instead of the usual "let's get it over with" slouch, they were listening and responding. I was able to trace some of these changes in attitude to a particular class activity, an exceptional student, and a lesson I learned from my students.

Picture Books

"You're reading a baby story!" shouted Paul.

"Shut up, it's easy," admonished Tom. It was the first day of school. My hands shook as I tried to appear confident reading *Teacher from the Black*

Lagoon, a picture book by Mike Thaler, to a class of juniors and seniors. I sensed that some students would need to be reassured that this was only a beginning and that the texts would become more challenging.

"Give me a chance to finish," I said. "If this is a really bad experience, I promise that I won't read any more picture stories!"

"OK, OK, I used to like these things. Go ahead and finish," Paul replied.

As I finished the story I observed their expressions. Most were curious, others amazed. I had just read, to a group of seventeen- to twenty-year-olds, a *picture* book. Before the shock wore off I asked them to think about the first time they felt afraid of going to school. If they couldn't remember, then they could think about a time when they were afraid of something that seemed very important but later realized it was their own imagination that scared them. I took a deep breath. "Now write about your experience for the next five minutes."

Write? There was the proof of the pudding. *Write* is a dirty word to vocational students. I expected complaints and perhaps rebellion. But, strangely, there were no complaints. One student even asked if he could write as much as he wanted.

And so it continued every time I read from a picture book. Sometimes students would look through the class library and choose what they would like me to read to the class or to read for themselves. I thought they would keep choosing picture books, but they would also select narratives, works of favorite authors, or even notable literary novels. There was never dissension over writing about the memories each book resurrected. What was even more amazing to me was the diversity their writing revealed. Simple stories triggered memories of parents and teachers, of grandparents whose death left empty pockets in the heart. Some of their writing actually pinpointed the exact time in their life when they became "at-risk" students. One student, after hearing Josephine Nobisso's book, *Grandma's Scrape Book,* wrote about the loss of her father.

> *It was his birthday. My sister and I did the silliest thing. We made cut out pictures and colored pages of our coloring books and wrapped them up as presents. We were to little to go to the store by ourself. Grandma picked us up and took us to daddy's house. We decorated with paper chains and baked the most awful cake! We waited and waited, but Daddy never came. It wasn't like him not to come. He loved us. Then the phone rang and Grandma came back crying*

in the room. She told us our Daddy was dead. He was in a motorcycle crash. I really loved my Daddy. I'll never forget that day.

When we talked about her writing, she said that life was never the same after her father's death. She hated everything. She went on to say that she never really thought about how her life had become so negative until she started remembering during writing sessions in English class. These sessions not only turned out to be therapeutic for other students as well, they also became a springboard to other meaningful writing projects.

Every two weeks I asked students to choose a piece they had written from their notebooks and work at completing it for a graded project. (In my old lesson plans, this same assignment was given to them in a handout that read, "Choose something to write about that means something to you. For example, you may write about a hobby, a friend, or a favorite vacation. The paper must be two pages in length, double spaced, and written on one side only." Generally, I would receive perhaps six out of ten papers, and these would be contrived, short, and contain very little detail. The four students who did not turn in papers would choose to fail because they "had nothing to write about." But the picture books got my students writing and some were asking if they could hand in two papers (one for extra credit!). Most surprising was that the writing was better than usual.

Soon, however, the picture book activity became routine. It was easy, the structure was predictable, and the writing was good because it came from their hearts. But that's as far as it ever went; these students would not write without some kind of prompt. When I refused to read a picture book or give them an assigned topic, they refused to write.

I could see from their efforts that they could write and would write—sometimes. I still did not know how they viewed their own writing, so I asked them for help. I distributed a survey with questions about how they wrote, their successes and failures, their strengths and weaknesses. The question they answered in the most detail was "When given a writing assignment, how do you approach it?" Some students said, "I'm sure I'll fail"; others, "I don't know how to begin." Only one said, "I look forward to it." The survey also revealed that spelling, grammar, and "nothing to write about" were their biggest problems. Finally, and most distressing, not one reported any strengths in his or her writing. Tom wrote, "I hate writing. It's dumb. I write when I have to. I don't know what to write. My gramer an speling are bad. I can only write if I have feelings." For years, these students had been told they could not write because they made too many mechanical and grammatical mistakes. Chucky, one of my automotive students, proclaimed, "You're the first teacher to read my story and not give me an 'F' because of all the misspelled words."

From the survey I learned that these students needed to be accepted at their current learning ability level and that they had a different way of functioning in the classroom. However, even though my students talked openly and quite frankly about their likes and dislikes, only one seemed objective enough to understand why some students were better at certain projects. She became my door to understanding what lessons they would learn—and what lessons they would tolerate.

Tammy

"The Complicated Direction"

Tammy had all the usual characteristics of a vocational student except one: she wanted to get good grades and graduate. She wrote on her survey, "I don't know how to begin. I am worried about the grammar, spelling and mechanics. I feel strongly about what I write." She was convinced that she *could* read and write, but she would only read and write what was necessary to get a good grade. Tammy attended class regularly. She found the writing and reading responses fun and, at first, she did the work necessary to receive an A and no more. Then, slowly, when the others would write a paragraph, she began writing pages. She wouldn't hand in a paper unless it was perfect. For the rest of the class one rewrite was enough; Tammy did many rewrites. She claimed that the other students only wanted the skills to get by in life, but she wanted to succeed.

Her greatest revelation was the result of a lesson called "The Complicated Direction." The class was divided into groups; each group was to choose a simple set of directions and write out each step. When students had accomplished this to their satisfaction, they were to substitute more complicated words using dictionaries and the thesaurus for help. This was intended to be a painless, fun lesson to increase vocabulary. All the classes enjoyed the activity so much that we published each class's revised directions and voted on which class came up with the most frustrating yet workable directions. Several students referred to their work experiences and how, many times, they found directions confusing. It was the first time they recognized that their vocabulary deficiencies could be causing work-related problems.

But for Tammy this little lesson had broader and more meaningful implications. Later, when she was to hand in a writing project, she asked for an extension of two days. Having a student ask for an extension when I knew the paper was complete intrigued me, so I gave her the extra days. What she turned in was amazing. Handing me her assignment, she said, "I'm really proud of this paper" and stated that the "complicated direction" lesson had moved her writing from competent to college level. Her eyes smiled as she continued, "You can show it to those teachers that teach college prep classes. Don't tell them who wrote it. Let them read it. Then shock them!" She was so proud. I followed her suggestion. The college prep teachers were impressed.

Tammy always made several drafts when she wrote, but then she would give her work a final touch: she would get resource books from the library and upgrade her vocabulary choices. Not only was her writing improving, she was increasing her vocabulary on her own. "That's crazy," stated one teacher. "We reinforce dictionary skills in the ninth grade!"— but with dittos and memorization. Such methods have no value if the student cannot use the words. This simple direction assignment's effect on Tammy was also a real lesson for me. For a student to value writing, the writing assignment must be meaningful. To learn vocabulary, the student must need the words and not just memorize them for quizzes or tests.

Poetic Responses

During the second semester Tammy asked if she could do a reading response in poetry form. Since I was exploring new ways to generate more writing, I agreed. Here is the poem she wrote in response to *How Does It Feel to Grow Old?* by Norma Farber:

Over the Hill

> *Over the Hill,*
> *out where the aches begin,*
> *where sexual desires,*
> *like smoldering fires,*
> *are replaced by martinis and gin.*

> *Over the hill*
> *to the land of cognacs and rum,*
> *where the beauties you chose*

are today's poster gals for Queen-size hose
and one day, no day, without Tums.

Over the hill,
*   at our Westinghouse celebration date,*
*   where, unfortunately it seems,*
*   so many of our own dreams,*
*   resulted in false teeth and Preparation "H."*

I had not considered the possibility of poetry for vocational students and it wasn't taught. If I had not invited my students to have a say in what we experienced as writers, Tammy's creative talents would probably have remained unexplored. It was at this time that I read *Emily,* a picture book by Michael Bedard. I asked students to sketch a picture of Emily Dickinson in words. Tammy wrote:

> *Emily is a very beautiful woman. The descriptions in the book put a lot of emphasis on her eyes. They seem to dance and twinkle. They're the color of Sherry, maybe a burgundy or plum color. Her hair is probably the same shade, some kind of burnt sienna. She is well kept. Her hair is always neat and never out of place. She may have a pale complexion from being inside so much. She may have been heavy, even though she was active, it wasn't enough.*

I brought some of Emily Dickinson's poetry to class along with two resource books about her life. Students selected three of Dickinson's poems and tried imitating her style. Tammy, instead, opted to write a poem to Emily:

Someone Special

Somewhere out there is a star
One holding your name.
It stands for your dreams—an inspiration.
It stands for your feelings which bear no shame.

It stands for courage and love,
and it sparkles a little brighter every day.

It stands for peace and all good
And it stays in one place—never to stray.

Sometimes it seems that the star has moved.
It seems as if the star isn't there.
But it is—for that star is really you,
Someone who follows that star—a person very rare.

At the end of the school year I asked students to complete an informal survey about the changes I had made in the Vocational English curriculum. Tammy's final remarks confirmed why change wasn't just good, but necessary: "I learned how easy it is to just sit down and write something, not anything, but something good!"

The Reluctant Auto Boys

There were a few students like Tammy in each of my classes, but the majority of my students had already resigned themselves to failure. One of these difficult groups was the "auto boys" (the boys in the Automotive Technology program). The auto boys observed that the Tammys were changing the assignments and getting good grades. So when it came time for the next project, they asked if they could write a cooperative paper. Jack, a muscular, second-year senior, asked, "Yeah, Mrs. T. This writing a short story sucks. Why not let us work as a group and write one short story? I bet it will be better than if we worked alone!"

Heads were nodding yes and the auto boys were smiling and clapping. Chucky, a very reluctant writer, spoke up: "Mrs. T, you know I write better when you give us a chance to work together! I make up great stories and Brad here can fix all my spelling." Brad then sat up straight and chimed in, "Yeah, and Matt can make the story exciting and Jack knows more about grammar than any of us."

Could it work? Why would the auto boys be able to write a paper together any better than they did on their own? To find out I investigated the automotive classroom where the boys spent most of their days. In the auto shop each student plays a special part in each project. In working with the automotive teacher, each student becomes aware of his or her unique talents: Chuck was good with brakes, Jack with gapping plugs, Matt with tools, Brad with front-end alignments. Together they produced a well-oiled machine. Together they helped each other with their cars. After listening to their conversations I also learned that they even planned their extracurricular activities together. I decided they could write the paper together. It took them two weeks, but when they were finished they had written a two-page story about off-roading. They were proud, and they added to their efforts by making a video of their off-road experience. There were still mechanical mistakes and some of the grammar had to be corrected, but the end result was a completed written assignment with a video as a bonus!

The remarks the auto boys made on their second informal survey were just as rewarding as Tammy's. Chuck defined good writing as "when you get a good story wrote that makes sense, and you get a good grade," while Matt said that good writing happens when you "write with feeling, description and good, good imagination." Brad's most fun projects were "the ones where you let us write about what we wanted. It was a lot easier writing about things that related to us!" And Chuck's most rewarding experience was "publishing my work in *The Power of the Mind* magazine" (written and edited by vocational students).

Even though the majority of my vocational students were reluctant learners, the changes in my English course gave all of them a chance to learn, to increase their self-esteem, and to set new goals toward success. From the writing surveys and interviews I learned that they preferred doing everything orally. They were very good at drills and skills, but they had been told for years, through the marks of the stern red correction pencil, that they couldn't write. By giving them a chance to write and being less critical of every mistake, I encouraged them to write. As I read their papers I tried to limit my focus to one or two writing errors. Because of their prior experience, the vocational students always worried most about mechanical errors and overlooked other aspects of writing related to meaning rather than form. Given time, students like Tammy flourished. She did go on to college, and at the time of this writing is maintaining a 4.0 grade average. But even the least-skilled students worked hard.

The best part of changing my teaching approach was the development of a writing community in which these vocational students could use their strengths to work together. Chucky, whose letter introduces this chapter, is a good example of what most of my vocational students are like. Although his future goals did not include college, he found the course valuable. Through writing these students discovered voices that were silenced in much of their other schooling and faced the future with more confidence, whatever career choices they would make.

CHAPTER 10

Roger, Jed, and Crazy Chris

Theresa L. McClain

Socrates, the wisest of teachers, said, "Know thyself." As the first after-noon bell rang, I watched twenty-eight students, mostly boys caught in that limbo between bicycles and driving permits, file into my room. I quickly moved the bigger and sweatier boys to the back of the room, well out of my olfactory range. The boys at our school inhale their food in ten minutes and then sweat at the hoop during the last twenty minutes of their lunchtime. Two of the boys stayed in close proximity. When I moved Chris back a desk, Roger convinced a girl to trade seats with him so that he could remain next to him.

I made a mental note that I would need more information on this pair. Both were decked out in concert T-shirts. "More heavy metal adolescents; I put in my time with this crew in the seventies as a novice," I thought. I in-troduced myself as a teacher/writer and assigned a small writing task. Most students took out their new pens and notebook paper and began to work on questions designed to give me both a writing sample and some back-ground knowledge to help me put names to faces. Roger began immedi-ately. Chris hesitated, and then started to write. Walking between the rows past his desk, I noticed that he covered his page.

Immediately, my training kicked in: "Share thyself." In *The Quality School Teacher,* William Glasser observes, "The better we know someone and the more we like about what we know, the harder we work for that person" (1993, 30). Students must feel safe, trust one another, and feel em-powered before they will attempt to produce good work. To create such a learning environment, the teacher must trust the students enough to share herself.

I stopped everyone and began again. This time I told students how important I thought it was to write. I mentioned that my father only had an eighth-grade education, which affected his earning potential and his influence in the world. "You will learn that I am a writer, in addition to working as a teacher. And much of what I write about deals with my family. Those are my children." I pointed to the picture of my son and daughter on the back file cabinet. Chris's eyes shifted to the back of the room. Referring to the vinyl writing portfolio in my hands, I added, "If you finish early, feel free to look through my portfolio. Now that you know more about me, I hope you will tell me about yourself in your writing." Chris did not look up again and hurriedly finished his assignment. When we passed the papers forward, Chris turned his face down.

When I read through the papers, I saw that Roger's was one of the best in the class. Chris did not share this glory; his paragraphs were choppy and of little interest. He had simply completed the assignment. The next day I returned the papers and noticed Roger smile as he read my penciled comments.

Workshop

This was the day I had chosen to introduce Reading and Writing Workshop. "We will not need our large red textbooks two days each week," I told them. "On Wednesdays and Fridays you may leave them in your lockers." I smiled as their eyes riveted on me. "I want to use a reading/writing workshop structure at least two days a week in our American literature curriculum. We will experiment with this approach." Roger listened. Chris grimaced.

"Tomorrow, I will give each of you a release form for your parents to sign. I am not in the business of monitoring the books you select, so the form will elicit your parents' help." Chris grinned at Roger. I anticipated problems with Chris's reading material, though as it turned out, I was wrong.

As I observed Roger, I had to admit that my initial judgment was incorrect. He was courteous. He worked diligently at all tasks and encouraged Chris to try. Eventually, in seventh period, I met their other friend, Jed. He wore a similar uniform, but he was more animated, nervous, wild. Every day he entered the classroom in a blast of sound, either mimicking an electronic guitar player, complete with the audio effects, or guffawing loudly over a prank he had just played in the hall. Although I knew his name, in

my mind I referred to him as the "Human Pinball." It would take extra effort to reach him. In the first week, after I had explained the reading workshop rules, Jed asked, "You mean I can choose what I want to read?"

"Yes."

"Cool."

Pleased, I recalled a recent *English Journal* article suggesting that students will read when they are allowed to choose material that is important
to them (Queenan 1996, 27). This policy seemed promising. At the beginning of each workshop, students from each group (five students per circle) distributed index cards to each student. Students recorded their name
on the card, the name of the book, and the page number where they began to read. At the end of reading time, I asked students to reflect on their
reading in writing and indicate the page number where they had stopped.
In his response, Jed mentioned that his friends Roger and Crazy Chris liked
reading workshop, too. In a journal entry, Jed mentioned that he and Chris
had become friends in study hall their freshman year. He said their pranks
would turn my hair gray.

Roger read mostly science fiction adventure stories; Jed was partial to
horror stories, the weirder the better; and Chris checked out a Poe collection from our class library. When he slept through the first two reading
workshops, he noted it honestly on his card. I initialed his note and wrote
back to him with a question about his story: "Why do you suppose Poe
was so mesmerized by his cousin's teeth?" Chris had to read a few pages
that period to have an answer, but he was able to stay awake long enough
to read until he found it.

Because of the writing communication time that reading/writing workshop provided, a relationship of trust was forged between myself and
these young men. Roger confided in an early journal entry, "Sometimes
people aren't as crazy as they may seem. They might just be misunder-
stood. The reason could, also, be that they don't receive enough attention
or support from family or other people. I know some crazy people, but
they are good people, and they're my friends."

In a flash, I headed for the gray two-drawer file cabinet where journals
are kept by class period. Students in my classroom understand the rules:
no one removes a journal unless he or she is writing in it, and no one reads
another student's journal or removes it from the drawer. This has worked
quite well for seven years. Quickly I found Chris's entry for that day:
"Roger and Jed are my best friends. Roger and Jed play guitar, and we want
to form a band." It was as if the three adolescents had collectively agreed
that it was safe to let me into their lives and said, "This is the day."

The next day, I ate in the cafeteria in order to observe the lunchroom cliques. Sure enough, as if in a fraternal society, Jed, Roger, and Chris were sitting at a table together. Roger, the nurturer, was studying his vocabulary list, and the other two were listening to his review. Another teaching truism, "Know thy students and know their friends," proved valuable. As a writing teacher, I realized that I could tap into their group dynamics by placing Roger solidly in my camp. His positive leadership and study skills would surely influence the other two boys.

Autobiography

For the first writing workshop, I had selected several prompts, but my personal favorite was an autobiography assignment idea I had borrowed several years before. I brought a finished example of autobiographical paragraphs I had written. The day before, I had asked students to bring in two pictures of themselves—one as a toddler and a current one. We began the writing activity by listing everything about ourselves we could think of related to that particular stage of our lives. We talked about toys, television shows, friends, games, and caregivers. We made lists.

Students shared their lists with other members of their writing group. Someone would mention *Dukes of Hazzard, Sesame Street,* or *Mr. Rogers' Neighborhood,* and the pen race would begin. Then I asked the students to draw a vertical line through the center of the page and make comparable lists for the past year. This seemed harder. "Wait," I pleaded, "I want to share with you something I read in a book called *Writing and Being.* The writer, G. Lynn Nelson, indicates that all good journal writing, even good public writing, comes from our feelings. Take your list now and revise it so that you can remember the year and reflect on your feelings about events. Make certain your list has heart and feeling."

When they had completed their lists and worked on sentences explaining that time in their lives, I asked them to share their pictures and their paragraphs with another person whose job it was to see if the paragraphs expressed feelings. We did not have time to finish the peer editing, so I told them that if they wanted, I would schedule a class in the school's writing center (an area of the library with thirty computers reserved for school assignments) to print the finished products. They voted to extend writing workshop another day to complete the activity.

In the writing center, Roger and Chris worked together. Roger motioned me over to them. "Chris doesn't have a preschool picture. They are at his mom's."

Both boys waited. "This is the writing you want to include in your portfolio for this nine weeks, Chris?" I asked.

He nodded. "I only see my mom now and then. I live with my father and stepmom."

"Fine," I answered. "Draw a picture that reflects the person you were then." He finished typing his paragraphs and moved to a corner of the writing lab with a piece of typing paper and a pencil. He was pleased when his autobiographical paragraphs and pictures were mounted on construction paper and displayed in the window of the library with the other students' writing for everyone to see.

I knew the barriers of distrust had been demolished when I read what Roger had written:

> *When I was a preschooler I was a completely different person from who I am now. Back then I was always playing with my brother and my cousin. My main concerns as a child were having all the coolest new toys. My room was a warehouse of new, old, and broken toys. My favorite toys were G.I. Joes. I had them all, and it was quite a collection. I also had my favorite Batman pajamas. They had a blue body suit and a cape attached with velcro. The most important adults in my life were my father and my grandparents. I played hide and seek with my cousin every night. Life was fun. Then I grew up.*

In his second paragraph describing his life as a fifteen-year-old, he wrote: "If my friends and I aren't listening to music, or if we're bored, we still play Hide 'N Seek at night. I think it is okay to play games now, because when I have a job and more responsibility there won't be any time for games." Roger knew in advance that his writing would be displayed in the library, yet he had revealed his heart.

In contrast, Chris's writing reflected little feeling. In fact, his sentences were only elongated and cleaned-up versions of his original prewriting lists. His writing group had pointed this out to him, but Chris was still in the "do-enough-to-get-by" mode. After a month of reading workshop, I asked the students to think about how they used this time. Chris wrote, "Reading always puts me to sleep. I figure I'm good for a page or two which is still more than I've read in other English classes since fourth grade." I made a note on his reflection card: "How about we compromise on five pages of reading per workshop?" He penned back, "OK."

Still, writing workshop and journals continued to offer Chris a place to talk about his life. His parents had divorced when he was in fourth grade. When his dad remarried, there was conflict, and Chris believed that his new mother thought Chris was stupid. "I set out to prove she was right, and nearly failed fourth grade," he confessed. There—it was out.

During the next writing workshop, I stopped by Chris's desk and knelt so that my face was at his level. I said I had read his journal entry and that I, along with other writers, believed that getting bottled-up feelings out in a journal was a great idea. "You don't say things that might hurt someone without thinking about them in print first, and getting it out is the first step in healing."

On his index card Chris wrote, "I have finally found an English teacher that likes me." For me, that was a red letter day.

MAC MAIL

In the fall I had read my English literature classes *The Jolly Postman,* a pop-up picture book filled with letters. Another teacher told me about her success with an assignment asking her students to write letters from one Greek god or goddess to another. So my classes wrote letters from any character in English literature to another character. The night before they were due, I painted a large cardboard box red and blue and stenciled the letters MAC MAIL in white on the outside. I cut a flap that lifted up and attached an old kitchen drawer handle. A postal employee friend loaned me an old postal uniform. I placed the mailbox outside the classroom, which created quite a stir in the halls, and students posted their envelopes in the box. Between periods, I slipped into my borrowed postal uniform and entered the classroom with the mailbox in my arms. With much drama, I pulled each letter from the box and read it aloud. Then students mounted their letters and envelopes on construction paper, and we bound them together with brads. Wisely, I had brought a camera and captured the experience on film. I wrote an article and sent it to the local newspaper. This created a problem: now every class wanted to use MAC MAIL.

My English 9 class MAC MAILed their vocabulary exercises to me on Mondays, and finally, near Valentine's Day, I purchased a stack of red construction paper and asked my sophomore students to bring buttons, lace, ribbon, yarn, and anything else appropriate, to decorate valentines. On the valentine, they were to compose a message from one American literature character to another. There were valentines from Hester to

Dimmesdale, from Ahab to Moby Dick, from Tom Walker to his money, and from Anne Bradstreet to her husband. One of my favorites was Jed's:

From Jordan to Nick:

> *Roses are red,*
> *Violets are blue*
> *I may cheat on golf,*
> *But I won't cheat on you.*

Roger, Chris, and Jed all completed this activity, and Jed's efforts were the most creative. Up to this point, Chris was still exerting minimal effort. In early March, however, as we finished reading *The Red Badge of Courage,* one of the workshop writing prompts hooked him. I had asked students to think about what it was like to be a soldier during the Civil War, to reread Henry's reflections in Chapter 2 if necessary, and to write a letter home on the eve of their first battle. While they worked in their writing groups, I played two Civil War tapes I had brought home from a vacation to Vicksburg and Gettysburg. Although Henry had been a Union infantryman, several students asked if they could write from a Confederate soldier's viewpoint. They posted their letters in MAC MAIL. Each group had to pick a letter from the mailbox to read aloud to the larger group. How pleased I was when both Roger's and Chris's letters were selected. Then I had one of those rare brainstorms: "Why don't we record the readings with the Civil War music playing in the background?"

The class was pleased. "Fine!" they said as I hustled to set up the equipment. After two failed attempts, I surrendered the job to a young man whose forte was electronic music equipment. At first, Chris hesitated. Collectively, the cry arose, "Just do it!"

Our musical producer told everyone to remain quiet during the taping process. Twenty-seven mouths clamped shut. The room was quieter than it had been all year, and I secretly prayed that the principal would walk down the hall and see twenty-seven students, mostly boys, diligently on task. Chris had written his letter to his dog back home:

> *Dear George, My Bestest Buddy:*
> *Hey, George. I'm a fixin' to go to battle. I just wanted to see if'n y'all wanted to accompany me to the front lines tomorrow. I know dogs can't read, but I can write. And I ain't got nobody to write to lessen you're a countin' Hector, the*

cat, and he ain't loud enough to answer me back. George, if'n I don't come back tomorrow, you and Hector can split ever'thin'.
> *Sincerely,*
> *Master Bob*

There was much to notice in Chris's letter, especially the poignancy of a soldier (or an adolescent) not having anyone to write to but his dog. The letter was well received by the students, who clapped enthusiastically when the entire taping session ended. Chris left the room talking animatedly to Roger, and when Jed came in during seventh period, he wanted to know why his class was drawing story murals when fifth period had gotten to write letters.

Reflecting and Evaluating

Before Christmas I had asked Roger if he would allow me to use several of his journal entries in a research paper. He appeared flattered, and I asked him to give me an answer after Christmas vacation. When I asked Chris, he chuckled "Yes," which indicated to me that all three had already discussed it. Obviously, this was a group decision, because Jed mentioned my research paper during seventh period.

Over the holidays, I reread many of Roger's journal entries. I was seeking ways to reach other boys like him: boys bound for trade schools after high school commencement, boys who preferred heavy metal music and guitar playing to English, boys from divided families who survived and still achieved in school, boys who were leaders of the peripheral cliques that operated within the school but weren't a part of the inner circle. In Roger's journals, I noticed repeated references to his grandfather, with whom he lived. He had indicated that his parents were divorced, and a permission slip I sent home to be signed by a parent or guardian had been signed by his grandmother. In his Thanksgiving entry, he mentioned eating at his mom's, his grandparents', and his father's homes. In another entry, he talked about owning guitars he had received as gifts at various times from his father, his mother, and his grandparents.

In the spring, I spent an hour talking to Roger during conference period. During this hour, I discovered that he and his half-brother had survived his parents' divorce. Both parents had remarried, and the boys had lived with their mother. When they were in middle school, his mother's new marriage began to fall apart, and she was forced to work long hours at her job to pay the bills. The boys had ridden the bus to their grandparents' to keep from going home to an empty house, and eventually they had simply moved in. His dad lived in a nearby town, and they talked frequently by phone, but Roger insisted with pride that his grandfather "can work harder than any man he knows," and bragged that his grandfather had worked over forty years at a local General Motors plant and usually only took five vacation days a year. He credited his desire to succeed, set goals, and offer support to his friends, to the stability of his grandparents' home, and to the work example of his grandfather. Roger knew that he influenced "Chris a lot and Jed just a little." Shyly he hung his head and grinned when he said, "I didn't do well at all in first and second grade because I didn't think my teachers liked me. It seems I always do well for teachers I like."

I admitted to him that I wasn't prepared to like him much at first. "I prejudged you and didn't think you would turn out to be a good student. I had to make an effort to learn enough about you to like you." He did not speak but nodded, acknowledging that he had understood this to be true.

Teaching assignments for the following school year were finalized near the end of May. I announced my schedule to each class. "Seems as if I will have two sections of English 11 next year." Led by Roger and Chris, the class cheered and clapped. Roger had finished the year with a B +; Chris had raised his last nine weeks' average to a C; Jed had managed to sit still long enough to pass the last nine weeks, although unfortunately not by a high enough percentage to redeem the first semester. But even Jed refrained from negativity. "See ya next year," he quipped when he learned his average.

Chris and Jed and Roger had become better writers and readers in that eight months. They had been allowed to read material important to them, to reflect honestly on their reading, and to develop a relationship of trust with me as a person and a teacher. Because reading/writing workshop freed me from the textbook, reading aloud, and lectures two days a week, I'd had time to read, write, and confer with students individually, to learn more about them. Writing/reading workshop had allowed us all to know ourselves better.

Afterword

Richard Bullock and Sherri S. Hall

Change is funny. On the one hand, we resist change. We find change uncomfortable and even frightening. We seem to long for security, familiarity, stasis. On the other hand, we insist that change is inevitable, a condition of life. Given the incompatibility of these two positions, we respond to the prospect of change in various ways: sometimes we embrace it, but other times we resist or ignore it. Our students change, our society's needs change, we change. Because change comes whether we like it or not, the question for us—and for our teaching—is, finally, do we control change or do we allow change to be forced upon us?

There is no shortage of people who want to tell teachers at all levels what to do and how to do it. Legislators pass laws, as they have in Ohio, mandating the teaching of phonics or establishing standardized proficiency tests. School boards react to one parent's pressure by forbidding the reading of certain books. Curriculum specialists tinker with course outlines. Principals are seduced by programs or fads. Hucksters for various educational programs and even entire schools abound. Parents complain. Students resist. In this Babel of competing, conflicting voices, teachers need to assert themselves to avoid being swamped by incompatible demands and to ensure that silence is not misread as acquiescence. Managing change must be done actively.

Once we've decided to take charge of what and how our practices will change, we still have to deal with the problems involved in doing so. We need to find ways to adapt our methods and materials to our sense of what is appropriate for our classrooms, our students, our communities, and ourselves. We need to find ways to initiate change that will not exceed our capacity to adapt, to feel comfortable with our new curriculums and our new classrooms.

One way to begin is to ask some questions:

Why do I do what I do now?
What really works for me and my students?
Why do these things work? What's the magic?
Everyone already does something really well; what do I do well?
What needs improvement?
What do I wish my students would do that they don't do now?
What can I do to get my students to do that?
Am I willing to fail?
Am I willing to succeed?
Can I give myself time to make change work?

These questions are the beginning of the journey—the adventure. But we need to recognize that although everyone starts with questions, we don't all come up with the same answers. In teaching, there are many ways to be right, and in our classrooms, we must be the authorities: no one knows our students and our teaching better than we do.

Dorothy Strickland, past president of the International Reading Association, has words of wisdom for teachers moving to workshop teaching: "First, be assured that you don't need to change everything overnight. Real change takes time." No one learned to teach traditionally overnight, so no one should be expected to change overnight, either. She also addresses the natural uncertainty that comes with attempting change. "Get used to living with a degree of ambiguity. You're really making progress when each question answered stimulates no more than two or three new ones" (1995, 301). Ambiguity permeates teaching, and with change, as with every other aspect of teaching, we need to define our practices for ourselves and to realize that new problems, new questions, inevitably arise.

The teachers represented in this book are convinced that workshop teaching is a better way of teaching than traditional ways. Their experiences, along with a growing body of research evidence, suggest that their conviction has merit. Yet, despite this growing evidence, other teachers, parents, and even students look on workshop teaching as suspect. How we respond to them is important. We need to be able to explain, as these teachers do, what we are doing and why. We should be able to throw open our classroom doors and proudly declare, "This is what we do here. Look! Isn't it wonderful!"

A Sample Workshop Course Plan

Stephanie Walter Corcoran

Overview

These materials were designed for a course I taught at Central Junior High School in Xenia, Ohio, a conservative, mid-sized town fifteen miles from Dayton. My course, Composition and Literature 9, was for freshman students of all ability levels. The course counted as one English credit toward graduation, and all freshmen were required to pass the course. Two years ago I moved to a different school in a different district, but my basic beliefs and course structure have not changed. I believe that in order for students to improve their reading and writing skills and to view reading and writing as important pursuits, they should read and write at school. My students spend their class time each day writing and reading within a predictable class schedule:

Mondays:
Writer's Chronicle (5 minutes)
Minilesson (5 minutes)
Silent Reading (36 minutes)

Tuesdays, Wednesdays, and Thursdays:
Writer's Chronicle (5 minutes)
Conferences/Silent Reading (15 minutes)
Minilesson/Exercise (5 minutes)
Silent Writing (21 minutes)

Fridays:
Writer's Chronicle (5 minutes)
Sharing/Groups/Reading (41 minutes)

Writer's Chronicle

Every day at the beginning of class, students write for five minutes on a given prompt (for example, a quote, a topic, a picture) in their writer's chronicle (see form 10). They should be doing this when the bell rings. The instructions for the chronicle describes its purpose: "Your chronicle will help you get into a thoughtful, creative mood, give you ideas for your self-selected writing, and help you develop your skills in the language arts." Student aides check the chronicles once a week, and students receive credit for each entry.

Minilessons

Minilessons are brief (five to ten minutes long) lecture/discussion presentations of information (see the list below) that students are expected to apply to their reading and writing. I tailor these lessons to the how and the why of writing: how to do a writing technique, for instance, and why it can improve writing. I follow minilessons with brief, guided practice, often done collaboratively, which I quickly check. I then instruct students to apply what they have learned to the piece of writing they are working on or to the book they are reading.

Procedural Minilessons:

How to check out books
How to head papers
On-task and off-task behaviors
Classroom policies
How writer's and reader's workshops work
How to do reading responses
How to do book celebration options

Reading Minilessons:

Selecting appropriate books
Genres
Literary elements

Author studies

Quaker readings

Colormarking poetry and stories for patterns, elements, tone, etc.

Vocabulary

Main idea, propaganda, functional reading, and other proficiency test
outcomes

Writing Minilessons:

Organization/Content:

Beginning/middle/end

Appropriate pace

Descriptive details

Description of setting

Description of action

Character shows emotion

Dialogue

Specific details

Sufficient details

Sensory details

Relevant details

Focus

Unity

Supporting details

Logic/makes sense

Paragraphing

Researching

Documenting sources

Style:

Lead gets reader's attention

Writing keeps reader's attention

Structure evokes emotions

Ending makes reader think

Writing has promises that are fulfilled

Creative approach to topic

Reader will find interest in topic

Varied vocabulary

Ideas expressed clearly

Title attracts reader

Purposeful word choice
Strong nouns
Strong verbs
Showing v. telling
Metaphorical writing
No unnecessary words
Realistic dialogue

Mechanics, Usage, Grammar, and Spelling (MUGS):
Correctly punctuated dialogue
Variety of (correctly punctuated) sentence structures
No fragments or run-on sentences
No no-excuse spelling errors
Correctly punctuated titles
Possessives
Spelling rules
Pronoun case
Subject/verb agreement
Consistency of verb tense
Correct use of verb forms
Pronoun/antecedent agreement

Reader's Workshop

Students are required to read silently in self-selected books each day; Mondays, for the whole period, and Tuesdays through Fridays for part of the period. In addition, they are expected to read for 30 to 45 minutes each night—this might be a self-selected book or a teacher-assigned reading, but it may not be homework for another class.

Students respond to their reading in a variety of ways: in-class reading responses and weekly reading responses of three or four pages, monthly book celebrations, class discussions, and book shares.

Writers' Workshop

Students are required to write pieces on self-selected topics throughout the year. They draft, confer, revise, edit, and publish their work. They maintain a writing folder and compile a portfolio of their writing. I evaluate this "showcase" portfolio quarterly, based on a rubric developed by the students. The portfolio should include four or five pieces each quarter.

Students are given a list of the types of writing they must include in their portfolios during the year. To ensure that students work toward completing their portfolios, they must hand in ten to twelve pages of writing each week. These pages are graded for completion and date-stamped.

Thematic Units

During the year, our class focuses on two thematic units, each lasting eight to ten weeks. Each thematic unit includes whole-class, small group, and individual reading, writing, speaking, and listening activities based on the theme. Our thematic units have focused in the past on Shakespeare and the Renaissance, centering on *Romeo and Juliet,* and Greek mythology, centering on *The Odyssey.*

1. Preparing for the Year: A Letter to Parents

Dear Parents:

This is the beginning of an exciting year for your child. We will spend our time together reading, writing, speaking, and listening. My research and experience over the past three years have reaffirmed my commitment to literacy and the role of reading and writing in personal growth and learning.

This year in Composition and Literature 9, your child will be participating in Reader's Workshop and Writer's Workshop. The workshop approach is an ideal way to provide each student with what he or she needs as a reader and as a writer. Our plan, based on current research in language arts, allows our students time to read and write, to claim their own reading and writing, and to respond to questions and ideas in both reading and writing. We will also be doing some collaborative and whole-class projects and reading this year.

Your child will be expected to read and write in class every day, and read at home for 30 to 45 minutes each evening as a minimum homework assignment. For Composition and Literature 9, your child will need to bring to class each day a three-ring binder, a 9 x 6 inch spiral or bound notebook, a pen and pencil, paper, coloring utensils, and a book they have chosen to read.

You will want to be aware that your teenager will be choosing not only his or her own reading material (books, not periodicals) but also his or her own topics to write about. You may want to help in this process by suggesting books, going to the library or bookstore, or suggesting writing ideas, such as an interesting editorial you run across in the newspaper. You might also encourage your child to read each evening, provide a quiet time and place to read and write, let your child see you reading and writing, and talk to your child about his or her reading and writing. Your level of involvement depends on your time and willingness, but the possibilities are unlimited.

You might also ask your son or daughter to show you the procedures handout (see form 1) on how the workshops work. The guidelines are very clear. Evaluation will be based on your son's or daughter's progress during the grading period. The grade rationale (see form 2) explains this fully; be sure to look this over with your child.

As your child's teacher, I need your cooperation and support so that your child will work at his or her fullest potential, which is, I'm confident, our mutual goal for Composition and Literature 9. If you have questions, concerns, or suggestions at any time this year, please write me a note. If this isn't possible, please feel free to call me at school. I am available at 555-0000 between the following times: 7:10–7:35 a.m., 12:25–1:10 p.m., and 2:05–2:40 p.m. If you must leave a message, be sure to leave a number where I can reach you during these hours.

Please write me a note acknowledging that you have read this letter and the course expectations, grade rationale, and discipline plan.

I'm looking forward to an exciting and successful year!

Sincerely,

Stephanie Walter Corcoran

P.S. There are a number of ways that interested parents can assist us. You may wish to consider the following suggestions:

1. Donating old paperback books or reference materials, or a book in your child's name.
3. Suggesting forums for publishing student work (office newsletters, competitions, etc.).
4. Volunteering your time to be a classroom aide, a lay reader, or a writing center tutor.
5. Donating supplies (white-out, paper, poster board, markers, crayons, glue, pens, pencils, scissors, pictures, postcards, posters, magazines, newspapers, old clothing, jewelry, accessories, hats for our "prop" box). We can use almost anything!

2. Communicating Expectations to Students: Handouts

Grade Rationale for Students

Each quarter's grades will be determined by your efforts, improvement, and achievement in the language arts.

Twenty-five percent of the grade will be based on your writing portfolio; 25 percent of the grade will be based on monthly book celebrations; 50 percent of the grade will be based on daily/weekly assignments.

Evaluation rubrics for portfolios and book celebrations will be developed in class.

Daily/weekly grades will include being on task during class, writer's chronicle, weekly reading charts (30 to 45 minutes of reading outside class daily), reading responses, self-selected and assigned writing, book shares, class discussions, monthly poems, and other individual, group, or whole-class projects.

After the first quarter, individual reading and writing goals will be determined for each of you and evaluated during an end-of-quarter evaluation interview.

Your portfolio grade will be based not on individual pieces of writing but on the body of finished work in your portfolio at the end of each grading period.

Note: If you are absent during Reader's Workshop, you are responsible for making up the 45 minutes of reading you missed by reading at home, during study hall, or after school in my classroom. You must fill out a reading makeup form and have it signed within a week of your return in order to make up points for reading. You may not make up reading during Writer's Workshop. In addition, every week you are responsible for your reading responses, your writer's chronicle, your 10–12 pages of writing, and all minilesson material and activities, regardless of absences, so be sure you take care of them. I will not remind you of your missing work! LATE WORK WILL NOT BE ACCEPTED FOR CREDIT!
Grades:

A = Work of excellent quality
B = Work exceeds minimum expectations
C = Work meets minimum expectations
D = Work falls below minimum expectations
F = Work done incompletely, incorrectly, or not at all

3. Materials Needed

You will need to have these materials by Tuesday, September [the start of the second week]. Bring them with you every day!

1. A three-ring binder with the following sections:
   • minilesson notes and handouts
   • writing in progress
   • reading response
   • word play
   • literature

   Everything in your notebook must be labeled, dated, and kept in chronological order. Your notebook will be checked for a grade (which will count as one week's grade) at our quarterly conferences.

2. A 9 x 6 inch spiral notebook or any size bound journal. This will be your writer's chronicle, which you will use at the beginning of class every day. Your writer's chronicle will be checked every Friday, and all chronicle writing must be in this notebook to receive credit.

3. A self-selected book that fits the theme/genre/unit of the month. This must be a book; it may not be a magazine or another periodical. You should be certain that the book you choose represents the content your family feels is appropriate for you.

4. A pen and pencil.

5. White, loose-leaf paper.

6. Crayons, markers, or colored pencils. (You may want to keep these in a plastic pouch in your three-ring notebook.)

7. *Writers INC.*, a writer's handbook you will receive from Mrs. Corcoran. This must be covered with clear Contact paper by Friday, September X. You should bring *Writers' INC.* to class with you every day.

4. Discipline Plan

Expected Behavior:

1. You will do only that which is helpful to your learning and the learning of others.
2. You will be in your seat, prepared for class, before the bell rings.
3. You will treat others with respect at all times.

Consequences of Positive Behavior:

1. Group activities
2. Letter/phone call to parents
3. Schoolwide recognition
4. Special privileges
5. Other

Consequences of Negative Behavior:

1. Conference with student
2. Removal from group or class activities
3. Phone call/letter to parents
4. Detention
5. Referral to counselor
6. Referral to assistant principal
7. Other

I agree to follow Mrs. Corcoran's expectations, and I understand the consequences if I choose to misbehave.

Signature _____ Date _____

5. Expectations for Reader's Workshop

1. Every day, you will need a book—not a magazine, a newspaper, or another periodical with pictures: these do not contribute to your fluency. You may read fiction or nonfiction, such as biography, history, etc. You may not read books of lists (which do not build fluency), and you may not read textbooks from another class.
2. You must read for the entire period.
3. You cannot do homework or read material for another class. Reader's workshop is not a study hall.
4. You must read a book. It can be fiction (novels, short stories, poetry) or nonfiction (histories, biographies), as long as it is a book that tells a story. Be aware that books with many pictures may not be acceptable if the pictures interfere with potential reading fluency. Reading materials for another class are not acceptable. If you have a question about whether your chosen reading material is acceptable, please ask me.
5. You must have a book in your possession before the bell rings to receive credit for preparation each day. If you need to go to the library or borrow one of my books, check it out before the bell rings!
6. You may not talk to or disturb others.
7. You may sit or recline wherever you like as long as you treat furniture with care (no feet!) and do not disturb others.
8. There are no restroom or water breaks to disturb me or other readers in the class.
9. If you are absent, you can make up the time and receive points by reading for 45 minutes at home, during study hall, or after school. You will have a week to make up reading after you return, but you must pick up a make-up form and have it completed. I will not come to you; make-up work is your responsibility. Also, free writes, reading responses, minilesson activities or information, writer's chronicles, and other work must be made up within the number of days you were absent in order to receive credit.
10. You will be expected to read for 30 to 45 minutes each evening and to write 3 to 4 pages responding to this reading each week. This reading might be self-selected material or material assigned by me. Material you read for another class is not acceptable. This reading will not count as make-up reading time if you are absent. Your weekly reading chart and 3–4 page reading response are due at the beginning of class each Monday.

6. Reading Response Assignments

You will be required to write 3 to 4 pages each week in response to reading done outside of class (30–45 minutes per evening). You should write each time you read, and record the response on your weekly reading chart.

Your responses should show your thoughts, opinions, interactions with the book/story/poems you read—I do not want a summary.

Some possibilities:

- interesting, provocative, representative quotes
- explanations of quotes
- letters to me, to classmates, to family members about the book (remember, no summaries!)
- letters to the author
- letters to the characters
- book reviews (like a movie review; not a summary)
- poems
- vocabulary discussions (new, unusual, fun words, how they're used, what they mean in the context of the story)
- discussions of the author's writing style, the characters, the plot (believability, excitement)

7. Monthly Books Assignment

You will be expected to read a book each month. You need to read one of each of the following genres this year, in any order:

- mystery
- history
- book of poetry
- courtroom/legal fiction
- romance/legend/myth
- fantasy/science fiction
- drama
- a "classic" work

1. One book must be written by a female author.
2. One book must be written by an author of an ethnic background different from yours.
3. One book must be nonfiction.

Note these books on your book log by number.

Options for Monthly Book Celebration:

Each book celebration will be presented orally to the class so we can share in the celebration. (You may do each option only once.)

1. A skit showing a scene (5–7 minutes per person receiving credit).
2. A poem summarizing the story (2–3 pages).
3. A sequel to the story (5–7 pages).
4. A cake depicting a scene (all decorations must be handmade by you).
5. A three-dimensional representation (all items must be handmade by you).
6. A collage (on full-size posterboard) representing the theme.
7. A videotape of a scene (5–7 minutes per person receiving credit).
8. A photo album representing the plot (20–25 pictures).
9. A story quilt representing the plot.
10. A newspaper (4–5 pages, typed, in columns). Your newspaper should include the following: sports article, news article, advice column, advertisements, comics, feature article, pictures, classified ads. All should be related to your book.
11. A game, with instructions and handmade pieces.

12. A slide show representing the theme and/or plot (5–7 minutes).
13. A song and dance (3–5 minutes per person receiving credit).
14. Advertising: a press release (1–2 pages, typed), a full-sized poster, and a new book jacket.
15. An oral "interview" of the author in person, on audio cassette, or on video (5–7 minutes per person receiving credit).
16. A wall-length mural depicting the changes that occur in the story.
17. A pop-up book (10–12 pages, each with a pop-up).
18. An audio tape that condenses your story, using actual dialogue from the story (5–7 minutes, 10–15 sound effects).
19. A treasure chest containing at least 10–12 items that represent the theme and plot of the story. Include a written inventory of the items and show how they relate to the story.
20. A mobile with at least 15–17 items that represent the theme and plot of the story.
21. A puppet show (5–7 minutes per person receiving credit).
22. A full-sized poster that depicts a character and uses 7–10 quotes from the book to describe the character's personality.
23. A series of 5–7 letters, each at least one page long, between the main character of the book and the main character of last month's book.
24. A graphic organizer (on full-size posterboard) depicting the plot of the story in the sequence of events.

You may do more than one book celebration project each month for extra credit as long as you complete all assignments for the quarter. Your book celebration grades will count for 25 percent of your reading grade each quarter.

8. Expectations for Writer's Workshop:

1. Write every day and finish pieces of writing.
2. Make a daily plan for your writing and work at it during class and at home.
3. Find topics you care about.
4. Take risks as a writer, trying new techniques and skills, with topics and and genres (kinds of writing).
5. Draft your prose writing in paragraphs.
6. Number and date every draft of each piece.
7. Maintain your skills mastery list and use it as a guide to your self-editing and proofreading.
8. Work hard at self-editing your final drafts and self-edit in a pen or pencil different in color from the print of the text.
9. Type final copies correctly, double-spaced with a one-inch frame margin.
10. Take care of any writing materials and resources with which I've provided you.
11. Make decisions about what's working and what needs more work in your writing; listen to and question other writers' pieces, giving thoughtful, helpful comments.
12. Work cooperatively with other writers in the classroom.
13. Do nothing that disturbs or distracts me or other writers.
14. Discover what writing can do for you.

What Writers Do:

- Rehearse (find an idea)
- Draft
- Confer on content
- Revise
- Confer
- Decide the content is set
- Self-edit
- Seek teacher-edit
- Publish

9. Portfolios

Your portfolio is a place to keep the collection of written pieces you will compose this year. Your portfolio will include pieces on topics chosen by you and pieces assigned by me. Your portfolio will be evaluated at the end of each quarter according to a rubric developed in this class, and the grade your portfolio earns will count as 25 percent of your grade each quarter in Composition and Literature 9.

Each quarter, your portfolio should include 4 to 5 finished pieces that represent your work that quarter. You may include additional pieces for extra credit as long as you have completed all assignments for the quarter.

This year, your portfolio must include the following types of writing:

- a poem
- a newspaper article
- creative nonfiction
- a fictional narrative
- a picture book
- research-based fiction
- a sonnet
- a research project

The topics of the pieces in your portfolio are your choice. Just be sure to avoid topics that aren't suitable for the classroom.

When it is placed in your portfolio, a finished piece of writing should include the following:

- a reflection: your thoughts on this piece of writing
- the portfolio draft, which must be typed and double-spaced
- the edited draft
- conference notes
- revision drafts
- the first draft
- at least two different types of planning strategies

Everything should be dated and labeled before it is placed in your portfolio. Only pieces you have finished should be placed in your portfolio.

During the year, you will not be permitted to take your portfolio out of the classroom, but you can take out individual pieces for a day. (You might want to make copies of pieces before you put them in your portfolio.)

You will be presented with your portfolio at a special ceremony at the end of the year.

10. Writer's Chronicle

Your writer's chronicle is where you will respond to quotes, works of literature, art work, music, and written prompts.

Your chronicle will help you get into a thoughtful, creative mood, give you ideas for your self-selected writing, and help you develop your skills in the language arts.

Your writer's chronicle is for school writing. It is to be used for intellectually creative thinking. It is not a diary. Do not write anything you wouldn't want others (including your parents) to read.

You must do your chronicle writing in your 9 x 6 inch notebook or bound journal every day to receive credit.

Your writer's chronicle will be checked every Friday.

You should write about daily topics as soon as you enter the room every day. If you are absent, you will be expected to make up your entry by Friday. If you are absent Friday, your chronicle will be due the day you return.

You should write the date and title or topic of each entry at the top of the page, and you should start a new page each day.

Works Cited

Anderson, P., and R. Brent. 1994. Teaching Kids How to Listen. *Education Digest* 59, 5: 67–70.

Atwell, Nancie. 1987. *In the Middle: Writing, Reading, and Learning with Adolescents.* Portsmouth, NH: Boynton/Cook.

———. 1996. Hanging Out with Big Sis. *Voices from the Middle* 3, 2: 42–45.

Barickman, Joan Estes. 1992. *Schoolwise: Teaching Academic Patterns of Mind.* Portsmouth, NH: Boynton/Cook.

Bean, John C. 1996. *Engaging Ideas: The Professor's Guide to Integrating Writing, Critical Thinking, and Active Learning in the Classroom.* San Francisco: Jossey-Bass.

Beginning Writing Groups. 1991. Tacoma, WA: Wordshop Productions.

Bollinger, Karen. 1995. Classroom activity presented at Strategies for Teaching Integrated Language Arts Workshop, Wright State University, Dayton, OH, July.

Bratcher, Suzanne, and Elizabeth J. Stroble. 1994. Determining the Progression from Comfort to Confidence: A Longitudinal Evaluation of a National Writing Project Site Based on Multiple Data Sources. *Research in the Teaching of English* 28: 66–88.

Burton, Esther. 1995. Personal interview, March 2.

Calkins, Lucy McCormick. 1986. *The Art of Teaching Writing.* Portsmouth, NH: Heinemann.

———. 1994. *The Art of Teaching Writing.* New ed. Portsmouth, NH: Heinemann.

DeFord, Diane E. 1993. Learning Within Teaching: An Examination of Teachers Learning in Reading Recovery. *Reading and Writing Quarterly: Overcoming Learning Difficulties* 9: 329–350.

Dillow, Karen, Marilyn Flack, and Francine Peterman. 1994. Cooperative Learning and the Achievement of Female Students. *Middle School Journal* 26, 2: 48–51.

Eisele, Beverly. 1991. *Managing the Whole Language Classroom.* Cypress, CA: Creative Writing PR.

Elbow, Peter. 1973. *Writing Without Teachers.* New York: Oxford.

Fleischer, Cathy. 1990. Revitalizing the Classroom: Students and Teachers Researching Together. *English Journal* 79, 4: 105–6.

Fletcher, Ralph. 1993. *What a Writer Needs.* Portsmouth, NH: Heinemann.

Fox, Mem. 1993. *Radical Reflections: Passionate Opinions on Teaching, Learning, and Living*. San Diego: Harcourt.

Gartin, Barbara C., and Annette Digby. 1993. Staff Development on Cooperative Learning Strategies: Concerns and Solutions. *Middle School Journal* 24, 3: 8-14.

Glasser, William. 1993. *The Quality School Teacher*. New York: Harper Perennial.

Hall, Sherri. 1995. Adventures in Sherriland. Unpublished manuscript.

Hanson, Philip G., and Bernard Lubin. 1989. Answers to Questions Frequently Asked About Organization Development. In Walter Sikes, Allan B. Drexler, and Jack Gant, eds., *The Emerging Practice of Organization Development*, pp. 15-23. Alexandria, VA: NTL Institute for Applied Behavioral Science; and San Diego: University Associates.

Hargreaves, Andy. 1994. *Changing Teachers, Changing Times: Teachers' Work and Culture in the Postmodern Age*. London: Cassell.

Hubbard, Ruth Shagoury, and Brenda Miller Power. 1993. *The Art of Classroom Inquiry*. Portsmouth, NH: Heinemann.

Hunzer, Kathleen M. 1995. Freedom as Constraint in the Writing Process. Paper presented at the Annual Meeting of the Conference on College Composition and Communication, Washington, DC, March. ED 357382.

Johnson, David W., and Roger T. Johnson. 1991. *Learning Together and Alone: Cooperative, Competitive, and Individualistic Learning*. 4th ed. Boston: Allyn & Bacon.

Kiester, Jane Bell. 1993. *Caught'ya: Grammar with a Giggle*. Gainesville, FL: Maupin House.

Lensmire, Timothy J. 1994. *When Children Write: Critical Re-Visions of the Writing Workshop*. New York: Teachers College Press.

Manning, Maryann, and Gary Manning. 1994. Twelve Guidelines for Teaching Writing in the Middle School. *Teaching Pre K-8* 25, 3: 59-61.

McDonell, Kathryn M. 1995. Bravado: An I-Search Project. Unpublished manuscript.

Meat Loaf. 1993. Rock and Roll Dreams Come Through. *Bat Out of Hell II: Back into Hell*. MCA Records.

Murray, Donald M. 1985. *A Writer Teaches Writing*. 2nd ed. Boston: Houghton Mifflin.

———. 1990. *Shoptalk: Learning to Write with Writers*. Portsmouth, NH: Boynton/Cook.

Nelson, G. Lynn. 1994. *Writing and Being: Taking Back Our Lives Through the Power of Language*. San Diego: LuraMedia.

Parsons, Les. 1990. *Response Journals*. Portsmouth, NH: Heinemann; Markham, ON: Pembroke.

Queenan, Margaret. 1996. Whole Language Is Not a Room Arrangement; It's a Controversy. *English Journal* 85, 2: 26-30.

Rief, Linda. 1992. *Seeking Diversity: Language Arts with Adolescents.* Portsmouth, NH: Heinemann.

Romano, Tom. 1995. *Writing with Passion: Life Stories, Multiple Genres.* Portsmouth, NH: Boynton/Cook.

Sebranek, Patrick, Verne Meyer, and Dave Kemper. 1996. *Writers INC.: A Student Handbook for Writing and Learning.* Burlington, WI: Write Source and D.C. Heath.

Sikes, Walter. 1989. Basic Principles of Change. In Walter Sikes, Allan B. Drexler, and Jack Gant, eds., *The Emerging Practice of Organization Development,* pp. 179–86. Alexandria, VA: NTL Institute for Applied Behavioral Science and San Diego: University Associates.

Silberman, Arlene. 1989. *Growing Up Writing: Teaching Our Children to Write, Think, and Learn.* New York: Times Books.

Smashing Pumpkins. 1995. Zero. *Melon Collie and the Infinite Sadness: Dawn to Dusk.* Chrysalis Songs/Cinderful Music.

Sommers, Elizabeth. 1993. Student-Centered, Not Teacher-Abandoned: Peer Response Groups that Work. Paper presented at the Conference on College Composition and Communication, San Diego, April 1.

Stotsky, Sandra. 1995. The Uses and Limitations of Personal or Personalized Writing in Writing Theory, Research, and Instruction. *Reading Research Quarterly* 30: 758–76.

Strickland, Dorothy S. 1995. Reinventing Our Literacy Programs: Books, Basics, Balance. *The Reading Teacher* 48: 294–302.

Strickland, Kathleen, and James Strickland. 1993. *UN-Covering the Curriculum: Whole Language in Secondary and Postsecondary Classrooms.* Portsmouth, NH: Boynton/Cook.

Trelease, Jim. 1995. *The New Read-Aloud Handbook.* New York: Penguin.

Vacca, R. 1995. Personal interview, May 3.

Weaver, Constance. 1992. A Whole Language Belief System and Its Implications for Teacher and Institutional Change. In Constance Weaver and Linda Henke, eds., *Supporting Whole Language: Stories of Teacher and Institutional Change,* pp. 3–23. Portsmouth, NH: Heinemann.

Contributors

Cheryl H. Almeda: taught English for six years at Springfield North High School in Springfield, Ohio. She currently teaches at a local community college as an adjunct instructor.

Mary Anne Anderson: teaches seventh and eighth grades at St. Sebastian School in Akron, Ohio. Now in her eighteenth year of teaching, Mary Anne has been a regional coordinator for the Power of the Pen and participated with her students in a peer mediation program for conflict resolution.

Richard Bullock: teaches in the department of English at Wright State University in Dayton, Ohio, where he directs the writing programs and codirects the Institute on Writing and Teaching. He has edited two other books: *Seeing for Ourselves,* with Glenda L. Bissex, and *Politics of Writing Instruction: Postsecondary,* with John Trimbur and Charles Schuster.

Stephanie Walter Corcoran: teaches seventh- and eighth-grade English and Reading at Tri-Country North Middle School in Lewisburg, Ohio. In her eighth year of teaching, she also teaches in Wright State University's Institute on Writing and Teaching.

Debra Ciambro Grisso: teaches language arts to eighth graders at Northmont Middle School in Clayton, Ohio. Debra has taught for twenty years and has appeared in *Who's Who in American Teachers.*

Sherri S. Hall: teaches at Shadyside High School in Shadyside, Ohio. A teacher for sixteen years, Sherri currently teaches speech, journalism, mythology, English, and Basic Writing in grades 7 through 12. She is a Martha Holden Jennings Scholar and is involved in community theater.

Richard D. Hughes: has taught special education at all levels during his twenty-five years of teaching. For the past several years he has taught English language arts to eighth graders at Brown Middle School in Ravenna,

149

Ohio. He was selected as the Ravenna Teacher of the Year in 1990 and nominated in 1991 for the Ohio Teacher of the Year.

Merikay Roth Larrabee: the first teacher in Lake County, Ohio, to receive certification from the National Board for Professional Teaching Standards, teaches English 9-12 in Painesville, Ohio. She has been teaching for twenty years.

Paula Lochotzki: teaches English II and English IV (World Literature) at Notre Dame Academy, an all-girls high school in Toledo, Ohio. She has been a teacher for twenty-eight years and taught every grade from second to tenth and grade twelve.

Theresa L. McClain: has taught grades six through college in her twenty-one years as a teacher. She now teaches English 10 and 11 at Greenon High School in Springfield, Ohio. She has published two books with New Hope Press, *Never Too Late* and *Forever After.*

Suzanne E. Theisen: teaches ninth-grade college preparatory English, Intermediate Composition, and Speech and Debate and manages the Speech team at Stow-Munroe Falls High School in Stow, Ohio. She is in her eleventh year as a high school English teacher and in 1994 was Teacher of the Year in her school system.